Making the best use of Cons

Other titles from Longman

Directory of Trainers and Consultants in the Personal and Social Services by *Alan Dearling*

How to organise Conferences, Workshops and Training Events by *Alan Dearling*

Making the best use of Consultants

A Guide for
Statutory and
Voluntary
Organisations

Philip Hope

LONGMAN

Published by Longman Industry and Public Service Management, Longman Group
UK Limited, 6th Floor, Westgate House, The High, Harlow, Essex CM20 1YR,
England
Telephone: Harlow (0279) 442601
Fax: Harlow (0279) 444501 Group 3 & 2

First published 1992

A catalogue record for this book is available from The British Library

ISBN 0-582-09824-6

Printed in Great Britain by BPCC Wheatons Ltd, Exeter

Contents

Contents

· List of Figures

Chapter One – What is Consultancy?

Chapter Two – Being Prepared to use a Consultant

Chapter Three – Choosing a Consultant

Chapter Four – Agreeing a Contract

Chapter Five – Diagnosis and Information Gathering

Chapter Six – Feedback, Action Planning and Implementation

Chapter Seven – Evaluating Consultancy

Acknowledgements

'Making the best use of Consultants' is based on my experience of providing consultancy to voluntary and statutory organisations throughout the UK since 1985. Much of the content draws upon the experience and knowledge of consultants with whom I have worked or trained in Framework, voluntary organisations particularly Save The Children Fund and local authority social service and youthwork departments .

I would like to thank my colleagues for their ideas, criticism, support and patience. In particular I would like to mention Sarah Hargreaves, Kevin Ford, Tim Pickles and John Holt from Framework and Alan Dearling, Roger Smith, Chris Chapman and Diarmuid Kearney for their comments on the material.

My thanks also go to Jill Stock for her excellent typing and for helping ensure I met the deadlines! And of course to Allison to whom I'm married and my two children Nicholas and Anna for putting up with my absence and my worries.

A list of references is given in the Appendices but I would like to mention 'Flawless Consulting' by Peter Block — a book that has strongly influenced my practise and to which I make a number of references. It should be regarded as essential reading for all consultants.

And lastly I would like to thank Tim Pickles and Alex Stevens, Warren Feek, Larrie Reynolds and Framework for permission to use their unpublished material.

Philip Hope
Framework

PUBLISHER'S NOTE

References in the text are indicated by numbers in brackets; a full list is given at the end of the book. Figures 1 and 7 are adapted from *The Consulting Process in Action*, Second Edition, by Gordon Lippitt and Ronald Lippitt, published by University Associates Inc, San Diego, California, 1986.

How to use the book

'Making the best use of Consultants' is a resource to help you improve the quality and effectiveness of consultancy as a tool for managing change and improving practice.

It is a practical guide for staff and managers of statutory and voluntary organisations who are considering the use of consultants to help them in their work. The book is structured in the sequence that you might work through if you were currently thinking of using a consultant – with a summary of key points at the end of each chapter:

You could read the book in this sequence or dip into topics of most interest or concern to you. The key points at the end of each chapter provide a quick way to become familiar with the main issues for each step in the process.

The guide provides clear and direct advice on all aspects of consultancy.
Each chapter includes:

- Discussion about key issues
- Examples of consultancy practice
- Summary checklists and diagrams
- Key Points

In breaking down consultancy into its component parts or into a series of stages and steps, the guidelines make the process look very tidy. Regrettably it's never quite like that. The structures and stages described in each chapter underpin what is a messier process in reality.

The need for guidelines

There has been enormous growth in recent years in the number of consultants and consultancy firms in practice and, in particular, in the use of consultancy by voluntary and statutory agencies.

Consultancy was first used in the UK in 1926 but only really developed in the 1950s and 1960s. At that time consultants were mainly offshoots of recruitment and executive placement agencies but in the latter half of the 1970s and throughout the 1980s there has been a tremendous growth in the number of consultants and the size of firms offering consultancy services.

It has been estimated that in 1989 there were eleven UK business consultancy firms, each employing more than 200 staff; 300 firms employing between 10–200 staff; and over 4000 consultants operating as sole traders (1).

But there is very little information available for voluntary and statutory organisations about how to go about choosing and making best use of these mushrooming numbers of consultants. Framework was a part of that growth in the '80s and is a small group of consultants and trainers working in the public sector with a value base of social equality, empowerment and ethical practice. We believe that the most effective consultancy contracts are collaborative. Consultants should empower the organisations and staff they work with and ensure that the outcomes and results are owned by the participants. This book is designed to help you achieve that result in the contracts you develop with consultants.

Chapter one

What is Consultancy?

Definition and Roles

● A Definition

For most people a consultant is an expert. Consultancy is seen as the process of having someone with specialist expertise — knowledge or skill — to solve your problems for you.

This is a very narrow approach to what consultants offer and how they operate. In particular it suggests that you, the participants, don't have any expertise and that you can't solve your own problems — neither of which are good starting points for a fruitful consultancy relationship or outcome.

The first element of a wider definition of consultancy is that of giving some kind of comment, advice or assistance. This could be giving specialist information, assisting you to solve a problem, or simply be the consultant reflecting back what she sees going on.

The second element is that consultants are there to assist you to improve a situation—to take action. Consultancy is not about research for the sake of understanding but is about gathering information to decide what changes or action to take.

And the third element of a wider definition of consultancy is that the consultant has no direct control over what you, the participant, decides to do. The consultant is genuinely 'advisory' in their status. In short, consultancy is defined as giving comment, advice or assistance to improve a situation where the consultant has no direct control over the implementation.

● Roles Consultants can Play

Within the broad definition there are many roles that you can ask a consultant to play, from someone who recommends a particular course of action to resolve a problem to someone who gives non-judgemental feedback on behaviour they have seen in a team. These approaches represent two ends of a spectrum of activity that consultants might carry out, as summarised in Figure 1.

Most consultants will play a combination of these roles in any consultancy contract. The traditional approach is to use consultants because they have specialist knowledge on a particular topic. But as the brief description of each of these roles and the examples of what these look like in practice show, there is a tremendous variety of ways of using consultants to assist you:

Positional Advocate You ask the consultant to analyse the problem and to give clear suggestions on particular outcomes, values and direction.

> The consultant conducted a review of a counselling project and produced a Development Plan with recommendations about its future aims, services, management and fundraising strategy.

Process Advocate You can ask the consultant to suggest particular ways of doing things such as using certain methods of problem solving — but not to become an advocate for any particular solution arising from the use of that method.

> The consultant observed a meeting of an Arts organisation board and then suggested the way future meetings could be run. The consultant did not comment on the decisions made at the meeting, only on the process .

Information Specialist You can engage a person who through his or her special knowledge, skills and professional experience provides special-knowledge

Consultant's role	Objective Observer/ Reflector	Process Facilitator	Fact Finder	Alternative Identifier and Linker	Joint Problem Solver	Trainer Educator	Informational Expert	Process Advocate/ Positional Advocate
Level of Involvement In Problem Solving	High ──→ Low							High / Low
Style of Work	Non-directive ←──→ Directive							
Consultant's Behaviour	Raise questions for reflection	Observes problem solving process and raises issues mirroring feedback	Gathers data and stimulates thinking and interpretation	Identifies alternatives and resources for you and helps assess consequences	Offers alternatives and participates in decisions	Trains your staff	Regards, links and provides policy or practise decisions	Proposes guidelines, persuades, or directs in the problem-solving process

You — High / Low

Consultant

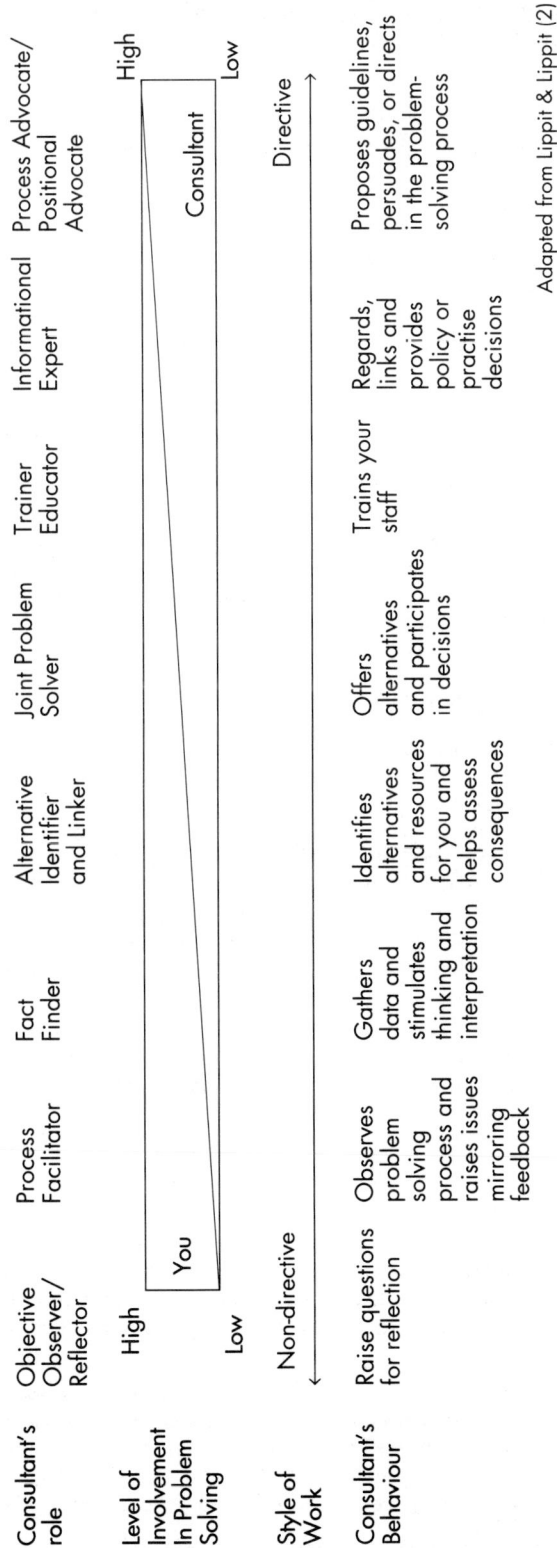

Adapted from Lippit & Lippit (2)

Figure 1: Multiple Roles of the Consultant

services. This may be to do with content concerning your particular problems or process on how to cope with the problem.

> In one case the consultant gave advice to a housing project on sources of funding for the agency. In another she gave advice to an organisation working with people with disabilities on how the organisation recruited staff in ways that ensured equality of opportunity.

Trainer/Educator   You can ask the consultant to design learning experiences or be a teacher. You may use training during a consultancy when you feel that a particular learning process is indicated in order for your organisation to acquire competency in certain areas.

> The consultant worked with a children's project to improve teamwork among the staff. As part of that process he ran a training day on supervision skills for all staff and managers in the organisation.

Joint Problem Solver   You can ask the consultant to collaborate with you in all the processes needed to solve a problem. The consultant may be involved in analysis and decision making as a peer but may, where conflict occurs, also assume the role of third party mediator.

> The consultant became a member of an inter-agency working party seeking to develop a new approach to responding to the needs of young people at risk of being abused. She offered professional advice on the practice issues and facilitated a closer working relationship between the different agencies involved.

Identifier of Alternatives and Linker to Resources   You and the consultant can identify alternative solutions to a problem; establishing the criteria for assessing those alternatives and the probable consequences of their implementation. The consultant can also link you to appropriate inside and outside resources. The consultant is not involved in the decision making.

> The consultant helped a staff team of a local authority to produce a joint report for a committee identifying options and possible resources for a new project on care for elderly people. In another example the consultant worked with a voluntary sports organisation to identify ways of resolving a financial crisis and getting expertise to help them with establishing sound financial management systems.

Fact Finder   You can ask consultants to use various information collection methods or fact finding techniques to assist diagnosis and problem solving. This is often an integral part of the consultancy process anyway where the consultant is functioning basically as an investigator. In carrying out this role the consultant will be intervening to some degree in your system and that itself will have an effect. The five basic methods are interviewing, questionnaires, observation, analysis of records and documents, and analysis of appropriate facts and data.

> The consultant interviewed staff from a variety of projects within an organisation about their work with homeless families and the future direction they would like to see the project take. The findings were reported back to a steering group to develop new ways of working.

Appendix 2 describes in detail a substantial consultancy for undertaking a strategic review of a community work organisation. This involved a combination of personal meetings, group discussions, questionnaires to staff and users, observations and statistical analysis.

Process Facilitator   You can ask the consultant to focus on the interpersonal and intergroup dynamics affecting the processes in your organisation/team. Process work may be involved in all the consultancy roles but a particular role exists for consultants who help you integrate interpersonal and group work skills with task oriented activities to support the improvement of relationships.

The consultant interviewed individually the 8 staff of a youth work agency and then spent two days with them to improve the roles within the group, management styles, inter-personal relationships and decision-making systems. The consultant then met the team for two further half-day review meetings.

Objective Observer/Reflector   You can ask the consultant to stimulate you towards some insights into growth or change, a discovery of a better method, or greater independence. This is the most non-directive approach. The consultant communicates none of his or her own beliefs and ideas to you and is not responsible for the work or the outcome. You are responsible for the direction chosen and reach decisions by yourself.

The consultant observed what happened during a night at a youthclub. The following day she met with the staff and some of the young people and asked reflective questions that helped people to clarify what had gone on, to confront the problems they faced and to make decisions about how to improve the youth club in future.

• Consultants are not Managers

Formal Authority   A consultant has no authority over the managers or staff in your organisation. Their advice can be completely rejected or ignored. You and other staff and managers cannot be made to do anything by a consultant. The relationship between your organisation and a consultant is a voluntary one.

If the consultant is given formal power over people in the organisation then the person is no longer a consultant. The authority relationship has fundamentally changed. The consultant has crossed the crucial dividing line between being a consultant and being a manager of the organisation.

A consultant is a person who is trying to have some influence over your organisation but has no direct power to make changes or implement programmes.

In one contract the consultant headed a team of youth work staff to develop new forms of practice.
The consultant and the team assessed the current practice, designed a new approach to running the project and got the principal Youth Officer in charge of the project to let him, the consultant, get the new way of working into operation.
The consultant was very satisfied with the result but it was the satisfaction of someone who has been a line manager — albeit for a short period. He wasn't really acting as a consultant but took over a bit of the line manager's job for a few months.

Informal Power   This is not to deny that the consultant has considerable informal power. The intrusion of an outsider will have considerable influence on your organisation. This can happen in ways that are empowering and supportive to you or feel intimidating and undermining. This is a key dilemma about making the best use of consultants and is a central, if not *the* central, theme of these guidelines.

> In one local authority the councillors found themselves on the receiving end of a report they didn't know much about and didn't agree with but felt it had to be implemented because they spent so much money on the consultancy. The way the consultant had carried out the task made staff highly anxious and the recommendations were not owned by anyone.
> Nonetheless, the report was implemented because of the informal 'authority' of such outside intervention.

● Consultants are not Inspectors

The Consultant's Role in the Organisation Consultants are often used and valued as independent and objective outsiders for evaluating pieces of work. However, they have no formal role in the power structures within the organisation.

Some people employed as 'inspectors' by central government or local authorities have a formal role in a decision making system. They may be part of the decision making process on questions of endorsement, funding or policy. The results of their inspections may be recommendations that the organisation cannot reject; their endorsement or lack of it will determine if something actually proceeds.

The role of 'inspector' in this way is perfectly valid and necessary but, crucially, you should not confuse this with the genuinely independent and objective role of consultants whose advice and support can be rejected without sanctions from another part of the decision-making system to which they belong.

Inspectors can act like Consultants It confuses matters that some people with the title 'inspector' choose to perform this task in a way that is more akin to consultancy. Some local authorities' inspectors, for example, often seek to help organisations to assess themselves and plan action for change. That is consultancy. If you work in this way with someone called an inspector, both you and they need to clarify this is what you are doing and establish the groundrules for working together in such a consultancy relationship. One such groundrule, for example, might be that, given their inspectorate role, information you provide to them may not be disseminated elsewhere without your prior agreement.

Consultants can act like Inspectors You can ask consultants to undertake evaluation of projects or pieces of work — they may give you support in carrying out a self-evaluation, work with you to carry out a joint evaluation or undertake an independent evaluation.

This third approach, independent evaluations, can in some cases be asking someone to inspect you — particularly if the consultant is asked to make judgements on whether the project or piece of work matches up to some external standards rather than achieving objectives or targets you set yourself.

Using a consultant as 'inspector' means she does not assist you to arrive at a judgement about something but that she will make this judgement and that you accept the judgement as the 'truth'.

There is no element of advising or supporting in this role — it is all about judging and justifying. This is a very limited form of consultancy. Whilst you may ask someone who calls themselves a consultant to carry out an inspection, both you and they need to know that it has considerable limitations. A different relationship will be created as a result — a relationship that is not about giving and receiving support and advice but a one-sided relationship in which the consultant has complete power to judge and determine the outcome.

The government funded a team of consultants to conduct an evaluation of a voluntary organisation. However, they were accountable to a joint committee of the organisation and the government department for that evaluation. The outcome met the needs and expectations of the organisation but not those of the government department. With hindsight what the government department really wanted was an inspection of the organisation for its own purposes rather than an independent evaluation of use to both organisation and Department alike. When the outcome did not match what it wanted, the government simply shelved the findings.

• Trainers can be Consultants

Members of staff attend external training courses to develop their individual skills, knowledge and attitudes. On return from the courses they may do things differently and may try to influence how others in the organisation operate. But the trainer's influence is limited to the impact they have on the individual.

Asking a trainer to deliver a training course to a group of staff within your organisation has a significantly different impact. Not only will each person develop as an individual, but inevitably issues will be raised and action identified about how the team and organisation as a whole operates. A subtle but significant shift occurs when what started as a training course becomes a means for examining and changing organisational policy and practice. Training has become consultancy.

On an open course on supervision skills and methods participants from a variety of organisations learnt what was meant by a supervision contract and improved their interpersonal skills in one-to-one supervision sessions. In contrast to this, in a course for a group of staff in one voluntary organisation, the trainees went on to draw up an outline policy for supervision which was then taken by the group through the decision-making structures. Staff on the course were at different levels in the organisation hierarchy. They worked for real on the issues affecting their working relationships. In effect the course had an organisation-wide rather than just an individual impact.

• Consultants as Non-Managerial Supervisers

A particular role that consultants often play in voluntary and statutory personal and social services is that of non-managerial or consultant supervisor. The consultant meets regularly (every 4–6 weeks) with a staff member or manager to provide individual professional or personal advice and support.

Crucially, the consultant provides *non-managerial* supervision and complements any line-management or peer support and supervision within the organisation (see Figure 2).

The advantages of consultant supervision as an addition to (*not* a substitute for) management supervision is that it can give additional personal support for people in highly stressful jobs, provide specialist professional advice, and focus purely on the development of the manager or members of staff as their consultant has no formal authority or control.

In one local authority the social workers in a multi-disciplinary team each used an external consultant for professional support on their different specialist area.

A Director of a voluntary agency used consultant supervision to gain personal support and specialist advice on ways of developing a team approach to their personal management of staff in the organisation.

7

Hierarchical
Supervision

Co-Supervision

Consultant
Supervision

Adapted from Payne and Scott (3)

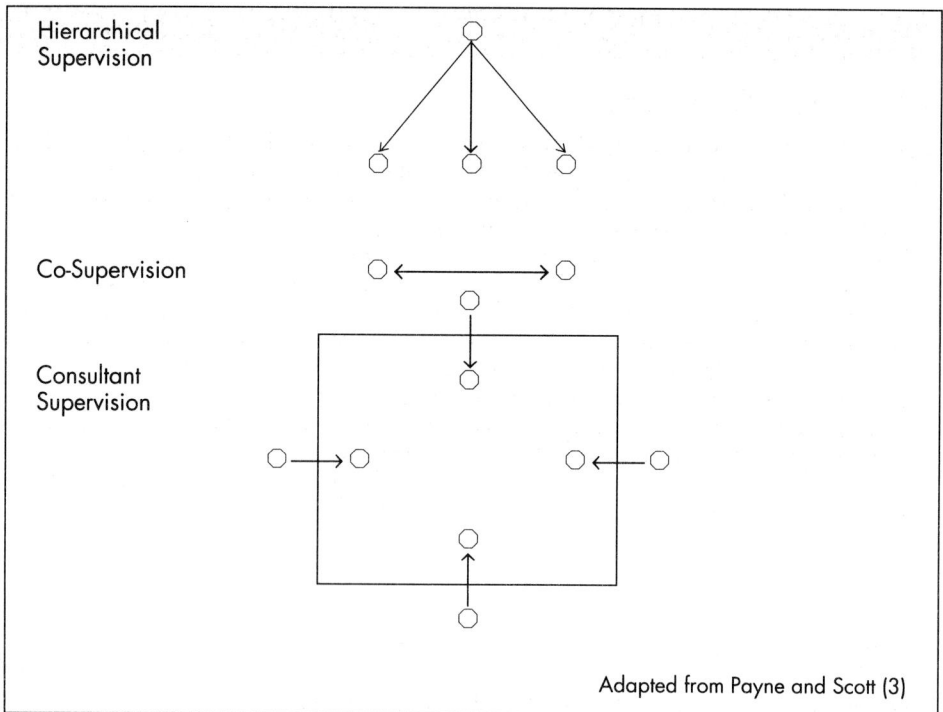

Figure 2:   Consultant Supervision

● Summary

A summary of the definition of consultancy, the roles consultants play and the overlap between consultancy, management, inspection and consultancy is given in Figure 3.

Definition
Consultancy is giving comment, advice and assistance to improve a situation where the consultant has no direct control over its implementation.

Roles
There are many roles a consultant can play from someone who recommends a course of action to someone who gives non-judgemental feedback on behaviours they have seen in a team.

Manager, Inspector and Trainer
Consultants are not managers – they have no formal power over people in your organisation.
Consultants do have considerable influence or informal power and how this is used is the key to making the best use of consultants.
Consultants are not inspectors who can impose sanctions on your organisation if their advice is not taken. However, inspectors can sometimes act like consultants and consultants can sometimes act like inspectors.
Trainers can become consultants when working with a group of staff from one organisation and using the training experience as a means of examining and changing organisations' policy and practice.

Figure 3:   What Is Consultancy?

Consultancy Principles and Values

• Value-Free Consultancy

The process of consultancy and the people who are consultants are *not* value free. Whilst some consultants may aspire to objectivity and independence, all consultants have values they carry with them. Rather than pretend to be value-free, consultants should recognise their values and declare them to you.

There are many underlying values that will affect the kind of role consultants play, the consultancy methods they use and the outcomes, if any, they recommend.

You need to be clear about the underlying values or principles upon which you want to base your relationship with a consultant. You need to be clear about how these might be reflected in the work the consultant does with your organisation. Codes of professional conduct have been devised by professional bodies representing consultants such as the Institute of Management Consultants, covering issues of confidentiality, independence, objectives and integrity.

Some of the key values or principles to be explored when using a consultant are given in Figure 4 and discussed below in great detail.

• Independence

You should avoid becoming *dependent* upon a consultant — or consultancy generally. The consultants you invite in to your organisation should be trying to work themselves out of a job. You and they should be dealing with issues in a way that prevents them from continuing to recur.

If you are always leaning upon consultants you are not becoming more able to do things for yourself. And consultants might also resist ending a relationship which makes them feel needed or gives them a secure income .

> One consultancy contract assisted a voluntary organisation to develop a new policy and structure for managing its youth work. Afterwards the consultant agreed to attend meetings of a key forum established in the structure. It became clear after three meetings that the consultant was not needed and that for the forum to work properly he should not be there. Agreeing to attend was really the consultant's need to be needed and the organisation's need for security. By raising this issue at the forum the consultant and the organisation were able to address it and mutually agree to let go.

• Empowerment

It is often the expectation that a consultant will arrive, solve your problem and then go away. But in effect this is him having the problem and the power—not you being empowered to solve problems for yourself.

During and after a consultancy you want to feel that your organisation is enhanced and that staff have the skills and confidence in what has been established to make things work well. Not only has the consultant worked himself out of a job but you and your organisation genuinely feel able to go forward with confidence.

Consultants who empower others do not seek power for themselves. They are consultants who are not keen to see their solutions used in preference to all others. They resist giving people answers but do ask difficult questions and raise unpalatable options. They do not spring surprises upon you and they do not operate in ways that undermine formal relationships.

Instead they build on strengths and provide you with experiences that enable you to work towards solutions for yourself.

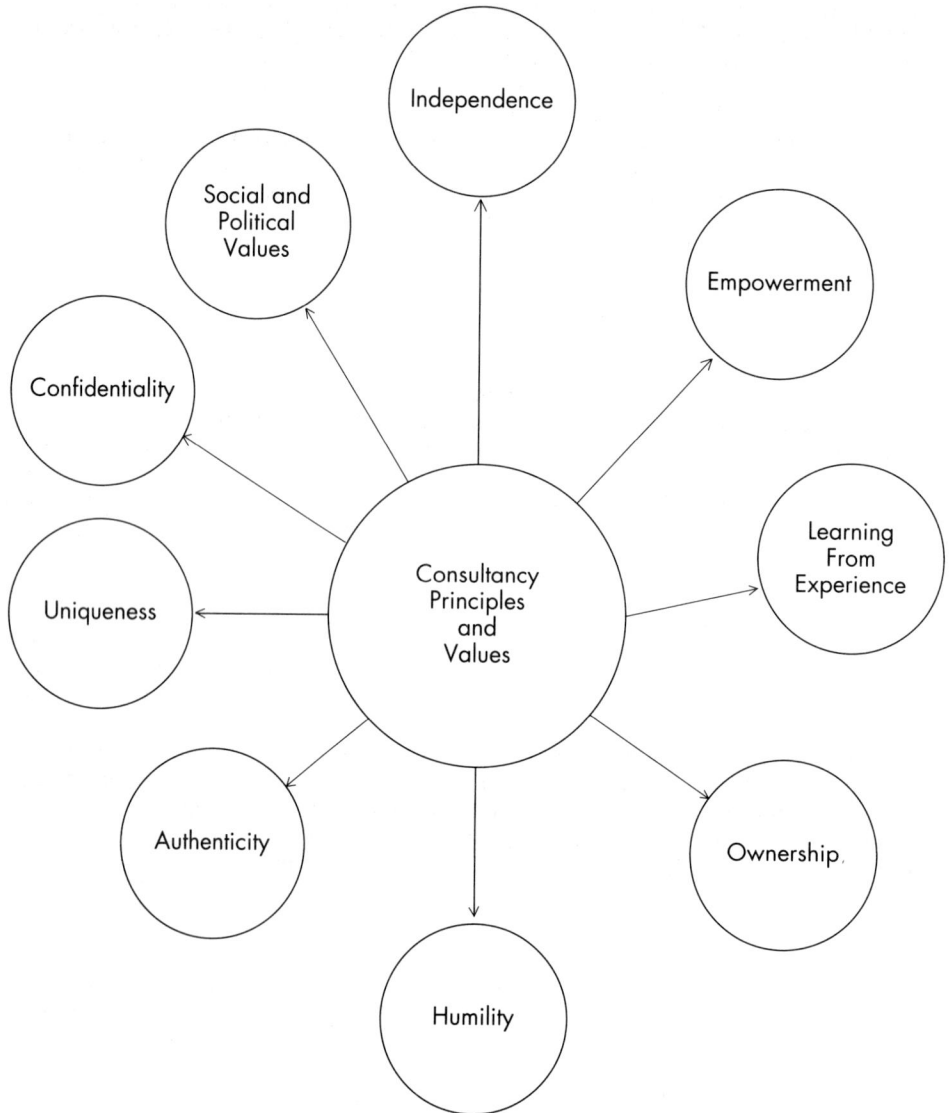

Figure 4:   Consultancy Principles and Values

At the end of a strategic review the consultant's final report included a recommendation for change that had not been explored in previous sessions. This left the staff and managers confused and uncertain about the way forward and suspicious of the consultant's motives. They assumed the consultant had been 'got at' by someone at the top of the organisation. The report was then used as a political football within the agency rather than as a valuable tool for change. The recommendations may have been sound but the way they were presented lowered morale and exacerbated the problems that the strategic review was designed to resolve.

● Learning from Experience

The most effective way people learn is from experience. This principle of learning from experience means that the consultant is learning from *your* experience in order to assist you to resolve a problem. It means consultants not simply coming up with options for change out of their heads but doing so from finding out from you what has been happening, what has worked or not worked, and what *your* perceptions are of your strengths and weaknesses. It means having a two-way dialogue to explore options and to enable solutions to emerge that are rooted in your experience and knowledge.

The principle of learning from experience also applies to the way you can learn from their experience as consultants. Whilst they can simply tell you what they know, it is much more effective if they can create experiences from which you develop that knowledge. This experience might simply be doing something differently in your work and reviewing how it went with the consultant. It might be a structured and participative exercise designed by the consultant.

Indeed, the consultancy experience itself — the way that you and the consultant relate to one another — is a rich source of experience to draw upon when analysing your approach to handling problems. You can design the consultancy to maximise your learning from the process. For example, in the initial stage of collecting information about an issue or problem, you can be directly involved in doing the interviews as well as being interviewed. You can work together with the consultant in analysing information and looking at options for change.

A group of staff wanted to improve how they ran meetings. They asked the consultant to suggest ways of running their meetings better. Instead, the consultant asked the team to discuss a real issue in their organisation and gave people roles to play such as always disagreeing with what another person said, or having a meeting-within-a-meeting. Although a simulation of the real event, it enabled participants to reflect on their behaviour, to give feedback to each other, and plan how to improve things in future. It also provided a common reference point for staff to relate to when similar things recurred in real meetings.

● Ownership

Consultancy is a process to help achieve change. Change is most effective when those involved feel they have contributed to or 'owned' what is going on. It is least effective when people feel that a change has been dumped on them. This often generates resistance, defensiveness and unnecessary anxiety.

You should seek to develop a collaborative relationship with consultants. This means not expecting consultants to solve problems for you but rather expecting them to use their skills to help you solve the problem yourself. And it means consultants helping you to develop a knowledge or skills they have so that you perform that task without them in future.

This means that you will be actively involved in gathering and analysing information and setting targets and objectives, and taking responsibility for the outcome.

It does not mean that you have to do all the work of the consultants, but that you work together in planning how the stages of the consultancy will be carried out, and carry out some of them yourself.

To be most effective in assisting change you should use consultancy processes that involve people and enable them to contribute to what is happening. Ensuring ownership of the consultancy through partnership means in practice:

- Involving all people directly at all levels in your organisation in the consultancy process.
- Establishing mechanisms for people to give comments on the conduct of the consultancy.
- Providing information to people about what has happened and what will be happening in the future.

The more the consultative process is collaborative and increases ownership, the better the chance for implementation after the consultant has left.

> In a review of the work of a voluntary agency the organisation was directly involved in deciding who should be involved in providing information. The consultant used the staff members' skills and experience to design the questionnaire. In another case the staff of a local authority jointly developed with a consultant a checklist for reviewing the quality of their work. They then applied this checklist and with the consultant planned action to improve their practice.

● Humility

The best consultants are humble. They do not try to prove how good they are as consultants but try to encourage you to recognise your strengths and skills.

Humble consultants do small things that matter, not big things that dazzle everyone. They avoid showiness and slickness but keep calm and ask basic questions. Humility is a consultancy principle that directly contradicts the conventional notion of the consultant being the expert.

" Trying too hard produces unexpected results:

- The flashy leader lacks stability.
- Trying to rush matters gets you nowhere.
- Trying to appear brilliant is not enlightened.
- Insecure leaders try to promote themselves.
- Impotent leaders capitalise on their position.
- It is not very holy to point out how holy you are.

All these behaviours come from insecurity. They feed insecurity. None of them helps the work.**"**

John Heider (4)

● Authenticity

'A consultant is being authentic when they put into words what *they* are experiencing when they are working with you' (5). Authenticity is a central principle of consultancy.

For example, if consultants feel you are treating the consultancy as a clever manoeuvre to sort out a problem they've created, the non-authentic consultant's response might be to negotiate to ensure the consultancy process is as open and participative as possible. But the authentic response would be for the consultant to say 'It feels like you're treating this consultancy as a clever manoeuvre to sort out a problem you've created'. The consultant may be wrong but in stating how it feels to him it focuses attention on the relationship between you and the consultant, closes the distance between you and builds trust. It means you establish a genuine relationship and pay attention to what is going on between you and the consultant. Such openness is essential to make best use of consultants. Working in that way will ensure that the underlying problems will be addressed and that your commitment to resolving the problem is reinforced.

> In working with a management team to review progress on action agreed at a previous session, the consultant felt the atmosphere had suddenly gone cold. Instead of frantically thinking about what might have happened, what he did wrong or what he might have missed in the discussion, the consultant said 'I feel the atmosphere has just gone cold. Do others feel this? Can someone say what has just happened?'

● Uniqueness

Your organisation is unique, so your needs will best be met by consultants who recognise that every organisation is different and who avoid simply imposing an 'off-the-shelf' set of solutions to your situation.

Consultants will have their own set of methods and theories, and will have their own set of experiences about what worked in other organisations. Some consultants specifically advertise themselves as experts in a particular approach. You need to be clear about whether you want consultants to introduce a particular method with a proven track record and to develop this within your organisation; or whether you want them to draw on a range of theories and practices to assist you to develop solutions to suit your situation.

> An organisation decided to introduce an approach called Total Quality Management. They chose a group of consultants who specialise in this, and worked with them to apply it appropriately within their organisation.

> An organisation was unsure about what approach would be best for them to maintain consistent standards in their work. They chose a consultant who offered a wide range of skills and methods to help them identify where the real problems lay, and what options there were for resolving them. The consultant then assisted the organisation to choose which option to implement and gave practical support to the staff in doing so.

● Confidentiality

The decision about what is confidential to the consultant and who will have access to the consultant's feedback or report needs to be understood and specified in the consultancy contract.

It is common, for example, for consultants to agree that what people say or submit to them will be confidential and made unattributable in the report or feedback. This encourages people to be more open in their replies and helps them to create a better analysis and more useful recommendations.

It must be made clear, however, what the consultant's position is if they discover illegal activities or working practices they believe to be seriously damaging to people. Only in certain forms of counselling is absolute confidentiality guaranteed. As with staff in your organisation, the confidentiality rule for information given to the consultant will not apply to illegal or seriously damaging practices. Feedback in these circumstances will be included in attributable ways with specific recommendations for action. If you fail to take action the consultant may reserve the right to take the information to the most senior level within your organisation or beyond.

Access to a consultant's report or feedback will largely be a matter for you to decide, although the consultant will want to negotiate that decision with you.

13

> A consultant working with a social services team on team development was seriously concerned about the practice described by one member of the team. She expressed her misgivings and recommended the individual to inform his line manager about what he was doing. The individual refused to do so. The consultant then told the staff member that she would inform the line manager herself but would prefer the staff member to do it himself or jointly with her. Eventually a three-way discussion was held between the consultant, the staff member and the line manager and the practice was changed.

● Social and Political Values

The consultants you use will have a set of social and political values that influence their work. These values will influence the work they do with you so be clear about what social and political values you want your consultants to have.

Choosing consultants with similar values may prevent a lot of mistrust about the consultancy within your organisation. It may also reduce the risk of conflict at the fundamental level of values between you and the consultant.

> An organisation working with people with disabilities and a commitment to social equality used a consultant to help them develop their staff recruitment and selection policies. They chose someone with experience of this aspect of management and who had demonstrated a commitment to anti-discriminatory practice and developing equal opportunities policies.

Whilst a shared value base will be of great help, you and the consultant will need to avoid the risk of 'collusion' whereby the consultant simply tells you what you wanted to hear.

It may also be beneficial in some circumstances to use consultants who do not appear to operate to your own value base. For example, you might wish to adapt the skills of planning, marketing or accounting of the commercial sector but to do so within a not-for-profit setting (6).

> A community work organisation used a marketing consultant from the private sector to assist its local community centres develop a public relations and marketing strategy. Some of the consultant's advice conflicted with what the organisation felt to be right, such as charging users for services they felt ought to remain free. But the 'market–led' way of viewing their organisation gave some new insights into the quality of the service they offered and ways of improving it.

Some consultants have as their starting point the view that unjust discrimination is widespread within society and organisations in the U.K. Consequently, when providing consultancy they will place an emphasis on gaining an understanding of the issues from the perspectives of people who experience such discrimination, particularly Black people, women and disabled people. This may be by meeting separately individuals or groups within your agency or by seeking the views of other organisations who offer these perspectives.

> A review of a youth work organisation included interviews and discussions with Black staff and Black agencies to gain an understanding of the Black perspective on the future of the service. The review included recommendations on the importance and mechanisms of ensuring continued representation of the Black perspective within the organisation. 'Black' was defined in a political way by the staff themselves as an inclusive term for a wide range minority ethnic groups who experience racial discrimination. It was a definition that the organisation wanted to see reflected by the consultants used to conduct the review.

- All consultants have values. These should be recognised and declared. There is no such thing as a value-free consultancy.

- Avoid becoming dependent on a consultant. They should be trying to work themselves out of a job.

- Consultancy should empower your organisation.

- People learn best from experience.

- A collaborative relationship with a consultant will increase the ownership of change.

- Consultancy is not about proving how good the consultant is but enabling you to recognise your own strengths and skills.

- Being authentic means consultants saying how they are feeling about what they are experiencing in their work with you.

- Your organisation is unique. You should be clear whether you want consultants to help you develop a specific approach to change.

- What you tell the consultant should be kept confidential unless agreed otherwise. But this groundrule should not apply to information about illegal or seriously damaging practices.

- Be clear about what social and political values you want your consultant to have.

Figure 5:   Consultancy Principles and Values – a Summary

Figure 5 gives a summary of consultancy values and principles.

Types of Consultancy Relationships

• Factors Determining Relationships

At the heart of a successful consultancy is a good consultancy contract. A contract is an explicit agreement of what you and the consultant expect from each other and how you are going to work with each other. When consultants are asked why things went wrong in a consultancy, they will often point to a problem in the original contract they agreed to. The process of selecting a consultant and agreeing a consultancy contract is crucial and is explored in depth in Chapters 3 and 4.

The nature of this relationship between you and a consultant can vary according to four factors:

1. **Status**   Is it a formal, written contract or an informal verbal arrangement?
2. **Time**   Is it a time limited relationship with a clear deadline; a relationship which is regularly reviewed at agreed time limits; or an open-ended relationship with no specified time limits?
3. **Structure/Phases**   Does the relationship have a clear overall structure with clear phases through which it is moving; or is there a structure and phases but only the consultant is aware of them; or is there no overall structure or phases?
4. **Aims and Methods**   Are the aims and methods for the consultancy task planned and agreed in advance; are they planned at the time you meet the consultant; or does the consultant just respond to events as they happen?

Using these criteria Figure 6 shows four main types of consultancy relationships and give examples of what these might look like in practice.

The choice of which type of relationship you develop with a consultant will be affected by:

```
                              FORMAL
                                |
  Formal and Planned            |    Formal But Ad Hoc
  • Written, specific contract  |    • Written, broad contract
  • Agreed, overt roles         |    • Agreed, overt roles
  • Clear structure and phases  |    • No phases or overall
    and time limited            |      structure — open-ended
                                |      time commitment
  • Work planned in advance     |    • Work done as planned
                                |      at the time
                                |
PLANNED ────────────────────────┼────────────────────────── AD HOC
                                |
  Planned and Informal          |    Informal and Ad Hoc
  • Verbal contract             |    • No contract
  • Roles recognised but not    |    • Roles are what they are
    formally negotiated         |      at the time
  • Structure and phases of     |    • No phases or structure
    the work apparent but not   |      — open-ended time
    written or discussed        |      commitment
  • Work planned in advance     |    • Respond to events as they
                                |      happen
                                |
                             INFORMAL
```

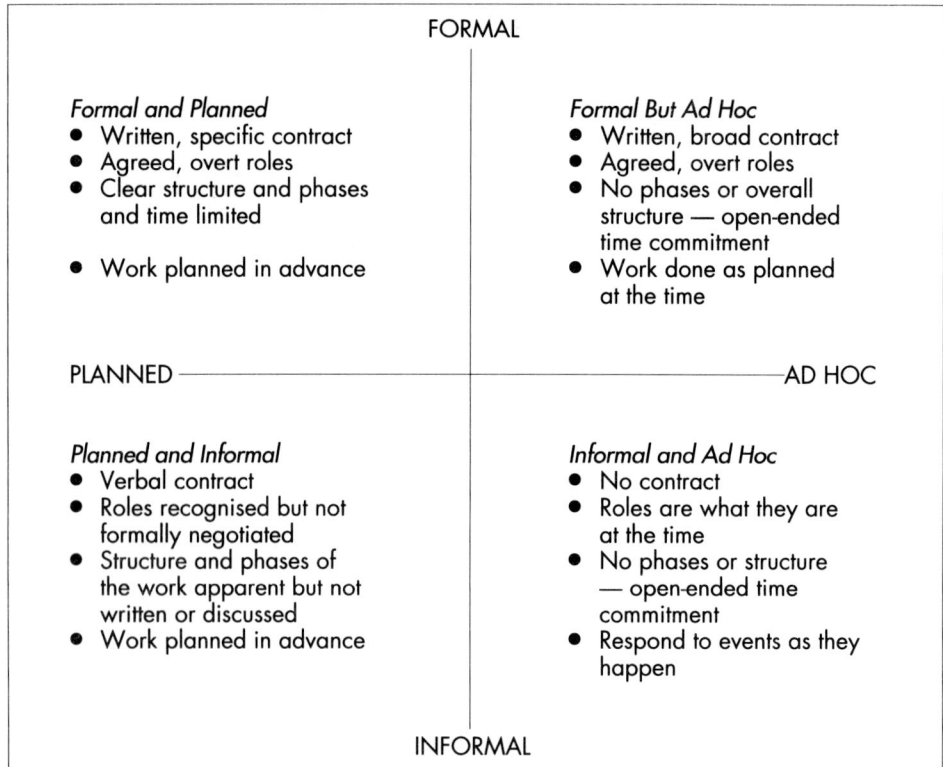

Figure 6:   Types of Consultancy Relationships

- The type of relationship *you* want with a consultant — your expectations.
- The type of relationship the *consultant* wants with you — their expectations
- The context in which you are working
- The nature of the consultancy task

• Formal, Planned Relationships

Most consultants working with organisations prefer a formal relationship of some kind with a written contract and clear, agreed roles. However, issues of time limits and structure to the work may be more or less negotiable according to the task and external constraints. A planned and formal consultancy relationship is often pre-ferred because of the benefits brought about in establishing clarity of roles and tasks; the practical need for consultants to organise their time well; 'cultural' factors that influence how consultants work; and the demand for such an approach within the organisations that are their clients.

The Benefits   In order to deliver effective advice or support to an organisation the consultant and you need to know what the consultant is expected to do and why, to know what the consultant is actually doing and how, and to agree when it is being done and what the outcomes are intended to look like. Without some formal agreement and some planning in the consultancy relationship there will be confusion and uncertainty. At best it could mean little of value will be achieved and at worst could mean that your organisation is seriously damaged.

Practicalities   Consultants will often be working with several organisations at the same time. They need to be clear about how much time they are spending with your

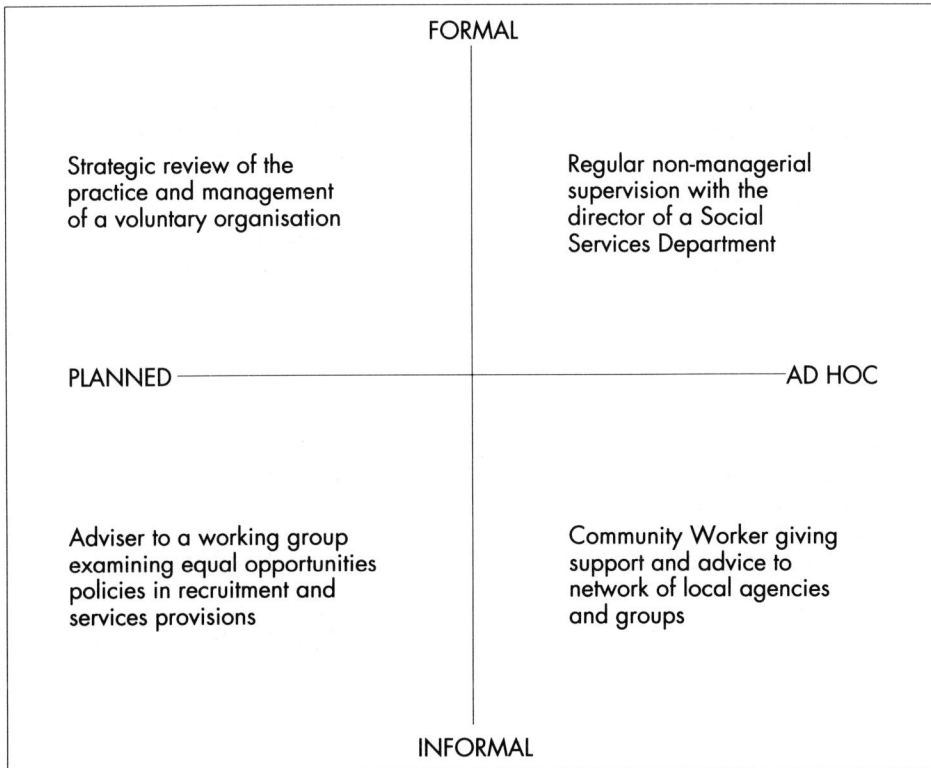

```
                              FORMAL

    Strategic review of the              Regular non-managerial
    practice and management              supervision with the
    of a voluntary organisation          director of a Social
                                         Services Department




PLANNED ──────────────────────────────────────── AD HOC




    Adviser to a working group           Community Worker giving
    examining equal opportunities        support and advice to
    policies in recruitment and          network of local agencies
    services provisions                  and groups



                             INFORMAL
```

Figure 6: cont.

organisation and to organise their diary to ensure they can provide you with the support and advice you want when you want it, and fit in their own preparation and thinking time. If they are being paid this may be done on a pounds per day basis and they will want to be sure they are giving the time for which you have paid.

Cultural Factors   Another set of reasons for choosing a particular kind of consultancy relationship may broadly be termed as 'cultural'. A formal, planned relationship reflects the management culture of the people and organisations with whom consultants work.

By contrast, this management 'culture' may not be appropriate to local communities where a community worker is seeking to assist people develop new initiatives or projects. A formal written contract may not, for example, match the informal culture of relationships between a community worker and the user groups of a local community centre. However, even in these circumstances the consultant should be clear with those with whom they work why they are there, who they are accountable to, what they offer, the time constraints and so on. This may not be written down but the community's acceptance of that person and the negotiation of their work and involvement with the community should be a formal and recognisable process.

It has also been suggested that the formal and planned consultancy relationship is rooted in a male, white and middle-class approach or 'culture' for doing things. As such it may not be an appropriate culture for particular groups of people, organisations or communities.

Consultancy styles that reflect cultural differences are important but do not justify

17

unplanned and informal consultancies. Having no structure in a consultancy leads to having no power. Promoting the principles of social equality and valuing cultural differences in consultancy can be done in ways that also ensure clarity about what is going on for everyone concerned. Such clarity may not end up as a conventional written contract but the key elements of a formal and planned approach can apply to a consultancy relationship within or between groups who may be of different culture.

The Demand from Organisations   The use of consultancy has grown enormously in the public sector in recent years. Many voluntary and statutory organisations now make regular use of formal consultancy and there are many more consultants offering their services in a contractual way.

Ultimately the choice of what relationship you establish with consultants will depend on what you and your organisation feel is appropriate for you and what the consultants feel is appropriate for them. The demand is clearly for more use of formal and planned consultancy relationships. This book is about improving practice in those types of consultancy relationships.

Stages in Using a Consultant

Your relationship with a consultant will develop through a series of eight stages from being prepared to use a consultant to finishing a consultancy contract (see Figure 7).

The first four stages are about deciding what you want to use a consultant for, selecting a consultant to work with and forming a contract for working together. These stages are examined in detail in Chapters 2, 3 and 4 and there are various long and short routes through them that are open to you.

Stages 5–8 are about what goes on during the consultancy and are to do with identifying and diagnosing the problem, gathering information, planning, taking action and completing the contract. The analogy of a hospital consultant is both helpful and unhelpful in understanding these stages in a consultancy. A hospital consultant gathers information about a patient, diagnoses their illness and prescribes and gives treatment. During the treatment the consultant regularly checks the patient and makes variations to the treatment. A point is eventually reached when the patient is cured, given different treatment or dies. The helpful part of this analogy is the phases. Organisations also get ill. They fail to work as well as they should and require treatment. The steps of that treatment can be equated with the hospital consultant's action in that it can involve:

- gathering information about the organisation;
- diagnosing the problems;
- providing advice and action to deal with the problem;
- reviewing how it's going and giving further advice and action and
- ending the relationship as your organisation is back on form again, or decides it needs other support and advice, or closes down (well, it had to be said).

The analogy can also be pursued in terms of preventive health care. Organisations can recognise that they may be about to enter a time of change or that by taking early action they can prevent a problem from occurring or being worse than it is.

The unhelpful side of the analogy concerns the image of consultants and the process of the consultancy. The hospital consultant is perceived as an all-knowing deity who will prescribe what is best for the patient. They are the expert on the human body so they know what is best. They will say what will happen in the

Stage 1:

> **BEING PREPARED TO USE A CONSULTANT**
> - Analysing The Problem
> - Deciding To Use A Consultant
> - Preparing A Consultancy Brief
> - Preparing A Consultant Specification

Stage 2:

> **MAKING CONTACT**
> - Identifying Consultants You Might Use
> - Making Initial Contact With Consultants
> - Holding Exploratory Meetings With Consultants
>   - readiness to change
>   - potential for working together

Stage 3:

> **SELECTING A CONSULTANT**
> - Inviting Tenders
> - Interviewing Consultants
> - Making A Choice

Stage 4:

> **FORMING A CONTRACT AND ESTABLISHING A COLLABORATIVE RELATIONSHIP**
> - The Process Contract
> - The Administration Contract
> - Who's Involved In The Contracting Meeting
> - Running The Meeting

Stage 5:

> **PROBLEM IDENTIFICATION AND DIAGNOSIS**
> - Collecting Information
> - Analysing And Diagnosing Problems

Stage 6:

> **FEEDBACK AND ACTION PLANNING**
> - Setting Outcomes Or Goals
> - Planning For Action And Involvement

Stage 7:

> **TAKING ACTION**
> - Taking Action
> - Evaluation And Feedback
> - Revising Action And Using Additional Resources

Stage 8:

> **CONTRACT COMPLETION**
> - Continuity And Support
> - Termination Plans
> - Evaluation

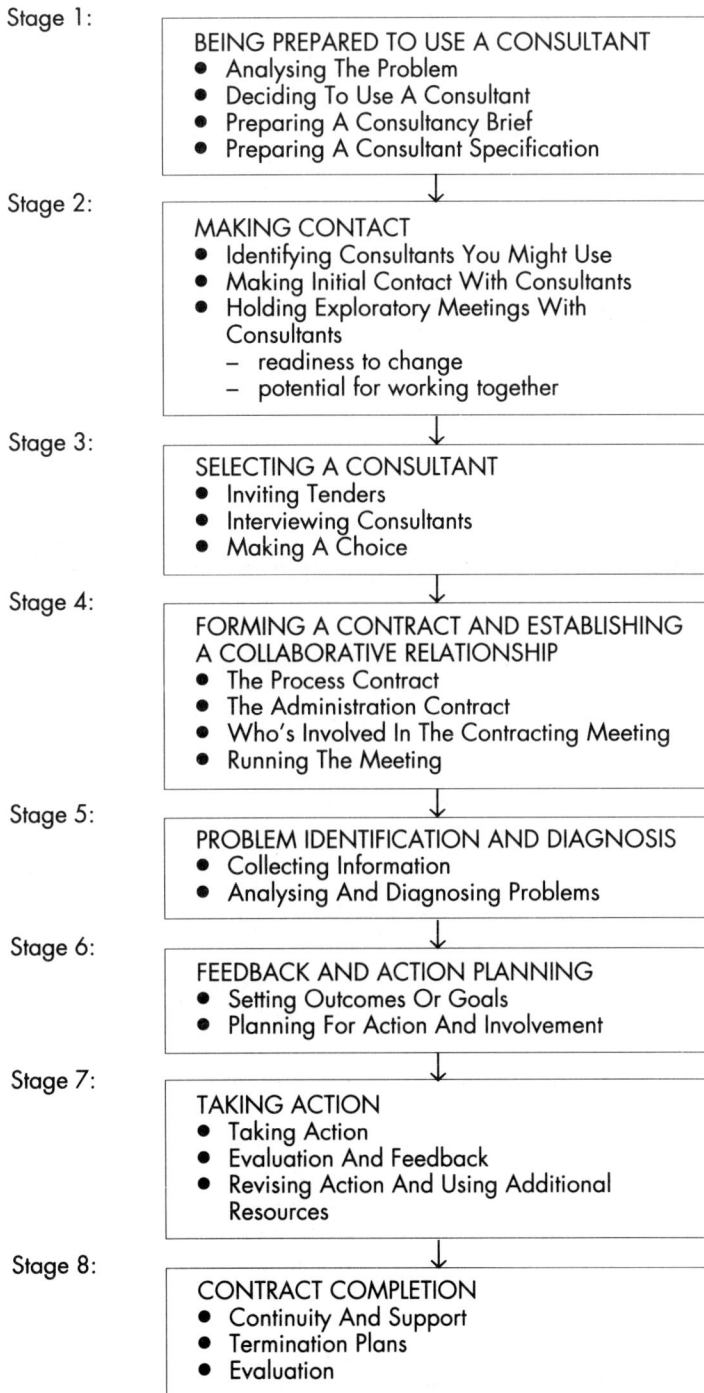

Adapted from Lippitt and Lippitt (2)

Figure 7:   Stages in Using a Consultant

medical field and are rarely challenged. This image persists and is unhelpful because good consultancy within organisations should reduce the all-knowing expertise of the consultant to a position in which their contribution is equal although different to the inputs of those involved in the organisation. It should involve a much wider variety of processes by which the consultancy can take place and pay attention to the involvement and support of people involved in the organisation. The 'doing' part of the consultancy (stages 5–8) is explained further in Chapters 5–7.

Internal and External Consultants

• A Comparison

Some consultants exist completely outside your organisation and primary networks. They are independent external consultants. Others may be staff members employed as consultants within your organisation or primary networks and viewed as internal consultants.

External Consultants The value of using external consultants is that they are:

- more likely to ask questions about basic aspects of the organisation that everyone takes for granted.
- less likely to be 'self-limiting' in their analysis of options for change and development.
- more readily acceptable as not having an 'axe to grind' as part of the politics of the organisation.

Internal Consultants By contrast internal consultants may:

- be directly 'in tune' with the organisation – its culture, ethics and atmosphere – as well as familiar with the basic structures and functioning of the organisation. They may be able to quickly grasp the particular issues of concern and to make more relevant diagnoses of how and where change might happen.
- be more readily acceptable (and credible) as someone who knows the organisation and supports what it is trying to achieve.
- know the internal 'politics' of the organisation.

• The Dilemmas of Internal Consultants

Internal and external consultants face similar dilemmas about their relationships to people with whom they work but do so to a different level of intensity. In choosing to use internal consultants it is worth bearing in mind that an internal consultant may:

- have specific organisational procedures that they want you to adopt.
- be under pressure to 'sell' the approach of their department to your department.
- be over-anxious about making you angry because the word would get round fast and put their whole job in jeopardy.
- have more limited access to key, high-level people when this is what they need.
- be given your trust and recognition more slowly because of the difficulty of being "a prophet in your own land".
- be limited by their own position/investment in the organisation as to the extent of change they are willing to consider.

Using An External Consultant
You ←——→ External Consultant

Straightforward relationship and negotiation of roles and accountability.

Using an Internal Consultant: A Triangular Contract
Consultant's Manager

You ←——→ Internal Consultant

More complicated 3-way relationship with need to recognise potential involvement and impact of the internal consultant's manager.

Using an Internal Consultant: A Rectangular Contract
Your Manager ←——→ Consultant's Manager

You ←——→ Internal Consultant

4-way relationship in which clear roles, expectations and accountability need to be established.

Adapted from Peter Block (5)

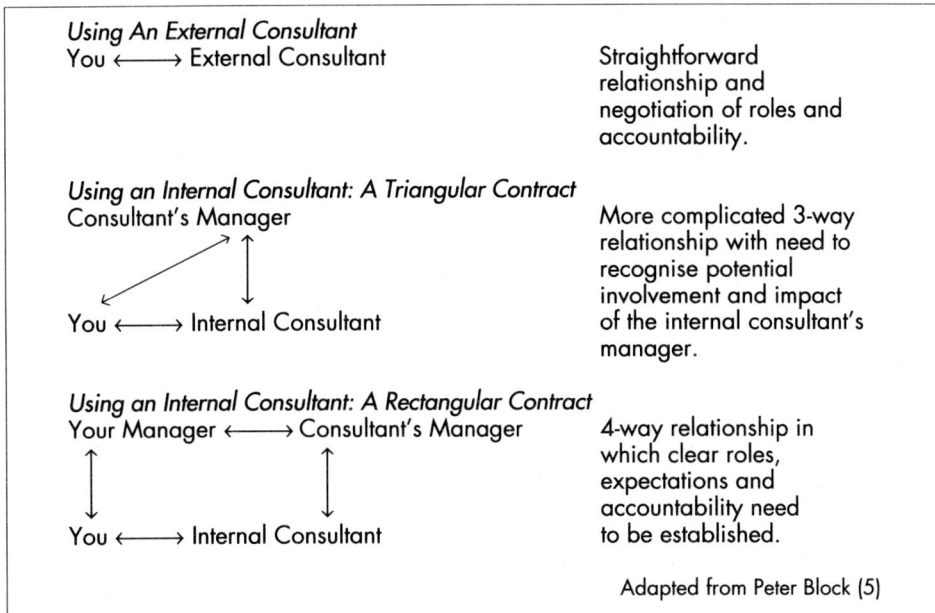

Figure 8:   External and Internal Consultancy Relationships

As a result of these pressures, internal consultants may feel more vulnerable and less willing to risk giving honest feedback.

In practice the use of an internal consultant will create a more complicated set of relationships to be negotiated as illustrated in Figure 8.

In the rectangular contract it is possible for you and the consultant to meet but be in a position where neither of you has given a commitment to begin. In effect this means you will be continuing to renegotiate and agree the contract.

WHAT IS CONSULTANCY?
KEY POINTS

- Consultancy is giving comment, advice and assistance to others to improve a situation where the consultant has no direct control over the implementation.

- You can ask consultants to perform a variety of roles or tasks to meet your needs. You should define and negotiate this with the consultant.

- Consultants are not managers or inspectors — they have no formal authority over your organisation.

- Consultants do have considerable informal power and influence in your organisation that you need to recognise and agree how it will be used.

- Trainers can become consultants if they train a group of staff from one organisation.

- There are a number of key values and principles that you should consider when considering the kind of consultancy you want: consultancy is not value-free; it should empower you and help you become independent, is most effective when based on your experience, will create most ownership if done collaboratively, is not about proving how good the consultant is but enabling you to recognise your strengths and skills, includes paying attention to the relationship you have with the consultant as well as the issue being addressed, and should be based on a clear understanding of the consultant's social and political values.

- The relationship you have with a consultant is best if it is formal and planned.

- Using internal consultants may require a more complicated negotiation of roles and responsibilities.

- Your relationship with a consultant will develop in a series of eight stages from being prepared to make use of a consultant to finishing a consultancy contract.

Chapter two

Being prepared to use a Consultant

What's the Problem?
- Different Problems and Consultancy Tasks
- Problems about how you deal with Problems
- Consultancy on how you deal with Problems

Defining your Problem
- Your Problem and how to tackle it
- Whose Problem is it?

Why Use a Consultant?
- The Benefits
- The Consequences
- Doing your Dirty Work

An Initial Consultancy Brief
- Budget and Timescale

A Consultant Specification

What's the Problem?

The decision to use a consultant suggests you have an identified problem or need and that external advice would help to tackle it. Before finding a consultant it is helpful to be clear about:

1) What you think the problem is, why it exists and how you want to address it.
2) Whose problem is it?
3) How ready are you for change?

The word 'problem' itself creates problems. It implies something is wrong with an individual, group or system which the project has to put right. This is often the reason why consultants are used but much of what goes on in voluntary and statutory organisations is about meeting people's needs, responding to external events or trying to improve what already happens. 'Problem' here is used as shorthand to cover problems, needs and issues — and is not necessarily something being wrong or at fault.

● Different Problems and Consultancy Tasks

You will, in the first instance, have identified a problem you want to resolve and for which you think a consultant might be able to help. This problem then defines, at least initially, the consultancy task you want undertaken. Indeed, there might not be an immediate issue but you might want to use a consultant to prevent a major problem happening. You might be aware that a change you are planning will create difficulties and you want to provide external support to assist people manage the process of change.

Some examples of problems and consultancy tasks within voluntary organisations and local authorities are given in Figure 9.

● Problems about how you deal with Problems

In helping you to resolve the 'technical' problems (fundraising, practice development etc.) consultants will want to examine and deal with issues about how you are dealing with that problem. For example, a consultant may give you advice on developing a new constitution for your management committee (the technical problem) but will also want to raise with you the fact that the chair of the committee and the Director of the organisation are not speaking to each other (how you are dealing with it). Indeed, this may be *the* problem to resolve and the 'technical' problem may be of less importance.

In order that you actually make use of any specialist knowledge that a consultant has to offer, you should expect them to raise issues they identify about obstacles to change to do with how you are dealing with the problems. These obstacles may be located in your working relationships, the way informal or formal power is used, personal management styles, attitudes to social equality and discrimination, inter-personal skills, mistrust between different staff teams and so on. You may feel this is none of their business. But if so, you will be preventing the consultant from doing her job and helping you to achieve the change you want. Whilst the 'technical' problem has technical solutions (eg. there will be an effective and appropriate way of supervising and supporting staff in your organisation), resolving issues about the way that this problem is being dealt with will have a greater chance of these solutions being implemented and having the outcome that is desired.

Focus	Problem	Consultancy Task
Review	We have been going for 5 years now and it's time we did a general review of what we've been doing and where we should go next.	Produce a 5 year Development Plan for the agency.
Planning	Our work is a mixture of reacting to events and pro-acting planning activities but we're all over-worked and can't decide on priorities.	Develop a new system for work planning and set priorities.
Evaluation	We don't know how effective the methods of a particular approach to practice have been and need to justify funding.	Undertaking an independent evaluation of a project.
Management Process	Staff and managers are feeling unsure about the systems and skills for giving supervision and support in the agency.	Developing a system for support and supervision relevant to our culture as an organisation.
Management Structures	There are overlapping roles and responsibilities and the current structure feels unwieldy.	Developing a new management structure with clearly defined roles and responsibilities.
Information	People are complaining they do not have the information they need to do their job.	Developing a new information system using computer technology.
Practice	The services we are providing do not seem to reflect our values of social equality and empowerment.	Developing new ways of working that put the values into practice.
Policy	The circumstances in which we work have changed and our policy now seems out of step with users' needs, other agencies' views and new legislation.	Developing a policy that reflects the changing needs of our users, legislation changes and the change in work of other agencies.
Public Relations	Users and other agencies are unclear about what we do and why we do it.	Develop a public relations strategy.
Finances	We don't have the information we need to make good decisions about our day- to-day spending or planning future budgets.	Develop a new financial information system for handling day-to-day accounts and creating budget forecasts.
Fundraising	Our 100% local authority grant-aid is coming to an end and we need to plan a realistic funding base for the agency.	Create a fundraising strategy.

Figure 9:   Different problems and consultancy tasks

In one contract an evaluation was commissioned by a funding body on the future practice and management of an organisation to which it gave a large grant. A report was produced that was well written and contained many useful suggestions. But the evaluation process failed to take into account the quality of the relationship between the organisation and the funders. By not addressing this problem during the consultancy, the report simply became another agenda item in the continuing argument and conflict between the organisation and the funder.

● Consultancy on how you deal with Problems

Indeed it is common for consultants to be used specifically on issues about how problems are dealt with because organisations have diagnosed for themselves that this is the problem that needs to be addressed. Staff teams often use consultants to assist them to improve the way they work together as a team. This directly focuses on questions of leadership style, the climate within the team, how people give and receive feedback to each other and so on.

Some organisations encourage staff to use consultants as non-managerial supervisors that give support and advice to individuals on how they handle problems rather than giving technical advice on the problem itself.

Defining your Problem

● Your Problem and how to tackle it

To be clear about *your* problem and how it could be tackled, work through the four planning steps below (7):

1. **Describe The Problem**   The problem or issue needs to be described so that people are clear and agreed about what it is they are focusing on. What does it feel like? How does it present itself?
2. **Analyse The Problem**   Once the problem is described it needs to be analysed. To ask: why does the problem exist? What is causing the problem? Answering this question is likely to have the most influence on guiding you towards ways of how to handle and ultimately resolve it. But it is also the most painful question. That pain highlights a difficult balance in preparing to use a consultant.

To what extent do you, the organisation, engage in asking these questions? And to what extent do you see asking them as being the consultant's role?

The people asking them might be a part of the problem but not realise it. And your self-analysis might be limited by your own bias towards a solution. Given that the diagnosis could be painful you should also avoid unnecessarily creating a bad climate beforehand.

Chapter 4 examines in more detail this 'diagnostic' stage in a consultancy contract. However, the greater the depth to which your organisation can ask and respond to these questions beforehand, then the better informed will be your choice of consultant and your brief to that consultant. Getting the balance right between asking these questions now and asking them with the help of a consultant is a choice you have to make.

3. **State The Outcome You Want**   It is important to be clear about what outcome you expect from the consultancy. What do people within your organisation want it to achieve? How, as a result of the consultancy, do you expect the problem to have changed? What will the new situation look like and feel like? These outcomes fall into two categories:

- Changes to the way you do things as an agency
  eg. – New ways of planning your practice
      – A new approach to supervising staff
      – A different way of fundraising.
- Changes that arise from changing the way you do things
  eg. – More effective use of staff time to meet user needs
      – Staff feeling more supported and more secure income.

But there needs to be a common understanding of the intended outcome if the consultancy process is to have the chance of success.

4. **Describe The Consultancy Method**   The final piece of preparation is to decide how you want the consultancy to operate. What role do you want the consultant to play? Who will they work with? What form will their intervention take and how will they feedback their findings? The nature of the problem, its causes and the outcome you want will give you some ideas about how a consultant might help you. The consultant too will have knowledge and experience about ways of responding to the issues and problems you are experiencing. He is likely to want to go through your analysis and your perceptions and add his own views and suggestions. The process of exploring the problem and agreeing a contract between yourself and the consultant is a crucial element in achieving a successful consultancy contract and is dealt with in detail in Chapter 4.

Figure 10 summarises this 4-step approach and gives two brief examples:

● Whose Problem is it?

Working through these four steps is itself making a start on the problem. In doing so you may find that some people feel the problem doesn't exist for them. Others will disagree about the analysis of what's causing the problem. You may find that people agree readily and already have ways of resolving the problem without using a consultant. You may find that what *you* are doing is part of the problem.

Involving a wide group of people in drawing up the initial brief for a consultant has a number of advantages:

- It helps to ensure you are working on the right problem and it might throw up other issues that need to be addressed.
- It helps to gain ownership among staff of the consultancy before the work begins.
- It begins the momentum for change.

The range of groups you consult and involve needs to be wide to ensure you see the problem from a variety of perspectives including:

- Black, women and disabled people
- Volunteer and paid staff
- Management committee members

The objective of working through the four steps in a way that involves others is to arrive at a shared agreement about the problem and the creation of an atmosphere of willingness to go ahead with some level of positive commitment. If that can be achieved, then the consultancy will be off to a very firm start.

Why Use a Consultant?

During this preparation phase you need to be clear about why you want to use a consultant. What added value will there be in involving a consultant? What will happen with the addition of outside support that you would probably not be able to achieve on your own?

4-Steps

1. The Problem/Need
A description of what the problem looks like and feels like now.

↓

2. Analysis/Diagnosis
A description of what you thnk is causing the problem.

↓

3. The Purpose Of The Consultancy
A description of the change you want to see.

↓

4. Consultancy Methods
A description of what you would like the consultant to do to help you achieve that change.

Example 1

1. The Problem/Need
The numbers of people using our service are going down and we only attract certain groups in the community and morale among staff is low.

↓

2. Analysis/Diagnosis
This is because our work is very traditional and has not changed to respond to changing circumstances. There is little 'new blood' in the organisation and many staff and volunteers have old-fashioned attitudes. We do not build on our strengths and have no real vision of where we are going.

↓

3. The Purpose Of The Consultancy
So we want to create new aims and methods of working that reflect today's circumstances, attract people from all sectors of the community, change staff attitudes and give a clear direction for the future.

↓

4. Consultancy Methods
To achieve this we will ask a consultant to conduct a strategic review and produce a report outlining a 5-year development plan for the agency that describes a clear statement of purpose and aims, outlines the methods and services we need to develop to achieve that purpose and describing new ways for managers, staff and volunteers to deliver this.

Example 2

1. The Problem/Need
Inter-personal communication poor and meetings go very badly.

↓

2. Analysis/Diagnosis
This is because people have poor personal communication skills, don't know how to run meetings and feel unsure about their new roles following restructuring.

↓

3. The Purpose Of The Consultancy
So we want more effective meetings, a better personal climate and more effective personal communication and behaviour.

↓

4. Consultancy Methods
To achieve this we will ask a consultant to do:
- A series of team building days for different departments including personal skills and role clarification exercises.
- A training session on running effective meetings for people at those meetings.
- A problem-solving session involving people from different departments.

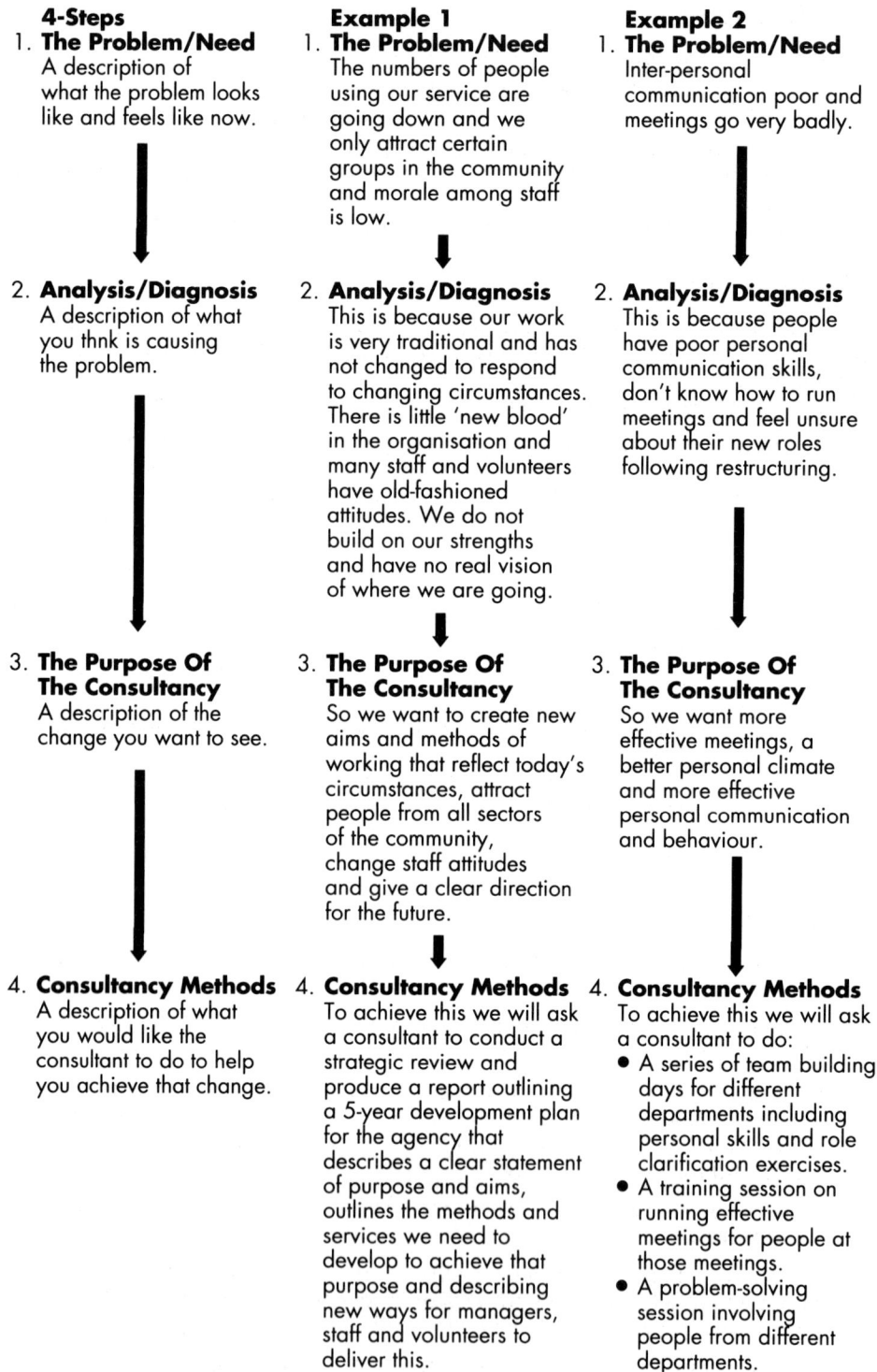

Figure 10: Analysing your problem and deciding how to tackle it

28

● The Benefits

The benefits of using consultants are that they:

- Bring additional expertise or knowledge on a topic you are unsure about.
- Have skills and techniques to ensure the processes of discussion and dialogue are constructive and achieve progress.
- Are not bound up by the relationships in your organisation – they are objective.
- Create momentum for change and ensure change takes place.

● The Consequences

Using a consultant will mean introducing change. You need to make a judgement about whether the organisation is ready for change, the level of resistance there might be, and the likelihood of success.

At a practical level this could, depending on the type of consultancy, include:

- ensuring there is agreement at management level for using a consultant and a recognition that this will mean change in the organisation .
- having or finding the money to pay for the consultancy.
- determining what staff time and resources you are prepared to put into the consultancy.
- agreeing an appropriate mechanism (such as a steering group) for involving staff from different levels of your hierarchy in the process of preparing a written brief, choosing the consultant, managing the consultancy as it proceeds and evaluating the outcome.
- agreeing the underlying values and style of consultancy you want to adopt.
- agreeing how everyone will be kept informed during and after the consultancy is completed.
- being prepared to use resources to implement change if necessary.
- being prepared to be challenged about how your organisation works.
- being prepared to air issues and concerns with an outsider even under strict rules of confidentiality.

● Doing your Dirty Work

Consultancy and consultants are viewed with great suspicion by some organisations:

" Management consultants often try to mystify their work and use complicated language that is difficult to understand . . . "

" At best they can provide some specialist technical information that the company may lack. For example, on new technology or health and safety. However, they are more likely to be asked to find ways of cutting losses and raising productivity ".

" Management consultants were brought in to compensate for weak management ".

" Employers used the consultants either to rubber stamp a decision they already wanted to take, or selectively by accepting only those parts of the consultant's work which they wanted ".

" Employers can also use consultants as cover for their own suggestions ".

Labour Research Department (8).

29

This highly critical view of consultants is rooted in trade unionists' experience of the use of management consultants. The Labour Research Department survey of their views makes for depressing reading and speaks volumes about the failure of organisations to manage change effectively. Using consultants to do your dirty work is an option that not only gives consultancy a bad name but says much more about your organisation and the way it operates and treats staff and users. A consultant with integrity will recognise what you are trying to do and challenge it. They may refuse the consultancy contract or refuse to continue it if your intent is deliberately mischievous. Similarly, organisations with integrity will recognise consultants who are pursuing a particular political agenda they disagree with and can challenge it or refuse to carry on with the work. The consultancies in the survey that attracted most suspicion and criticism were to do with organisations and methods, communication, work studies, staffing levels and privatisation or contracting out.

Ways that you and the consultants can avoid abusing consultancy when looking at these kinds of issues are:

- being honest and clear about the real purpose of the consultancy.
- being open throughout your organisation about the purpose and process of the consultancy.
- involving people from different levels in the organisation formally in the process through agreed structures and by involving the trade unions (where they exist).
- discussing the terms of reference of a consultancy with staff from different levels or with different personal perspectives and with trade unions. Agreeing for example an approach that asks consultants to identify ways of improving efficiency without loss of jobs.
- involving staff and trade unions in the choice of the consultant.
- agreeing open access to the findings and not binding the union or staff representatives involved to confidentiality, as doing so makes it very difficult for them to fulfil their role.
- agreeing a process for discussing and negotiating the findings of a consultancy including drawing up agreements on issues arising.
- using the consultants to help you examine why you find some decisions difficult to take and to help you develop better management skills to manage the process of change.

An Initial Consultancy Brief

The internal discussions about the use of a consultant should result in an initial consultancy brief (see Figure 11).

It is an initial brief because you should expect consultants to want to establish a mutual agreement on the problem you want to address and how to go about it. You should view your initial brief as a negotiable document in the same way as you would view a tender to carry out the consultancy.

An initial consultancy brief should give a summary of your organisation – its aims, methods and values; a description of the problem that has led to the consultancy and why you think the problem exists; the purpose of the consultancy and the outcome you want to achieve; an outline of how you think the consultancy might be carried out; an initial budget and timescale for the work (see below) and a specification of the consultant team you are looking for (see Figure 12 and related text, below).

● Budget And Timescale

You will need to include an initial budget (the amount you want to spend) and an

An initial consultancy brief should describe:

- a summary description of your organisation and values.
- the need or problem that has led to the consultancy and why you think it exists.
- the purpose and outcome you want to achieve.
- an outline of how you want the work to be carried out to achieve this.
- an initial budget and timescale.
- the consultant specification.

The consultancy brief should be no more than 2–3 sides long.

Figure 11: The Initial Consultancy Brief

initial timescale (the deadlines for starting and completing the work) in the initial consultancy brief.

Most consultants calculate their costs on a per-day basis. So one approach you can use to drawing up an initial budget is to find out a range of consultancy charges and decide on an initial budget based on how many days of a consultant's time the job should take. This will give you and the consultants you talk to a starting-point for discussion.

Consultants need to know the initial budget and timescale to determine whether they are interested and able to do the job. They will make an initial judgement about whether your budget is sufficient to pay for the number of days the consultancy is likely to take at the price they charge. Some consultants adjust their fees and tenders to match the budget because one large piece of work is more economic than finding, negotiating and carrying out a number of small pieces of work. Others have a range of fees according to the size and type of agency they work with (e.g. small voluntary organisations or large local authority).

You also need to be clear about how much money you intend to spend on the consultancy and when you want the work done. You may know at the start how many days of a consultant's time you wish to use — for example, your brief may say that you are looking for a consultant for two days to work with the management team on team development. Having found out some example of costs and drawn up a budget, you will then be negotiating with consultants how much you are prepared to pay for the preparation, delivery and writing up of those two days.

Alternatively you may only have a broad task in mind, some idea of the work you want a consultant to do and when, and a rough budget of the sum of money you think is enough to do it. Tentative though this may be, it will still give some very helpful indications to prospective consultants of the overall size of task you envisage and your timescales. If it is tentative, then you must expect consultants to want to negotiate the time and money with you — particularly if they feel you have underestimated the size of the task or omitted particular elements they feel are of importance to its success.

The question of money and time next becomes important when you are choosing a consultant (Chapter 3) and agreeing a contract (Chapter 4) .

A Consultancy Specification

Part of the preparation for using a consultant is to consider what kind of consultant you want. A consultant specification should outline the attributes you believe are essential for the consultant or team of consultants to have, as summarised in Figure 12.

- value-base:
  eg. a concern for social justice

- the skills required:
  eg. groupwork skills
      questionnaire design skills

- the knowledge required:
  eg. youthwork policy
      management theory

- relevant experience:
  eg. management experience in the voluntary sector

- position:
  eg. internal or external to the organisation

- personal perspectives:
  eg. race, gender, sexuality or disabilities

Figure 12:   Consultant Specification

It may be the case that the nature of the consultancy task requires the perspective of someone of a particular race, gender, sexuality or disability, or a consultancy team with a balance of personal perspectives. This can be made clear in the consultant specification. Depending on the nature of the contract you may deliberately choose to use an individual consultant or to use a group of consultants. Large pieces of work that cover a range of issues may be better undertaken by a team — for example, someone with financial analytical skills, another with knowledge of organisational structures and a third with experience of the practice base. On the other hand, a team development consultancy with a small staff group may best be undertaken by an individual with specialist groupwork skills.

You may not find a consultant or group of consultants who have the combination of values, skills, knowledge, experience, position and personal perspectives you want. You will probably have to prioritise which of these attributes are most important. It will always be the case, however, that you should ensure the consultant has the values and personal skills you believe are important for creating the kind of consultancy relationship you want.

BEING PREPARED TO USE A CONSULTANT
KEY POINTS

1. Before finding a consultant be clear about what the problem is, why it exists, and how you want to tackle it. You need to be clear about whose problem it is and how ready you are for change.

2. You will have an initial idea about the 'technical' problem you want to tackle. Consultants will want to help you look at how you are *handling* that 'technical' problem. Some contracts such as a team development consultancy focus solely on how you handle problems.

3. You can make an initial attempt at defining the problem you want to tackle by working through 4 key steps:

   1. Describe The Problem
   2. Analyse The Problem
   3. State The Outcome You Want
   4. Describe The Consultancy Method

4. When defining the problem you want to address, ensure you gain the views of a variety of people in your organisation — people with different personal perspectives or at different levels, volunteers and paid staff, users and committee members.

5. Do not use consultants to do your dirty work for you.

6. Prepare an initial consultancy brief that summarises the problem and how you want a consultant to assist you in resolving it.

7. Draw up a consultant specification that describes what kind of consultant (or group of consultants) you want.

Chapter three

Choosing a Consultant

Choosing a Consultant and Agreeing a Contract

Long Routes and Short Routes
- ■ The Long Route
- ■ The Short Route

The Selection Process
Step 1. Identify Consultants you might use
Step 2. Make Initial Contact with Consultants
Step 3. Hold Exploratory Meetings with Consultants
Step 4. Invite Tenders from Consultants
Step 5. Interview Consultants
Step 6. Make a Choice
- ■ Personal Contact
- ■ Written Information
- ■ References
- ■ Payment

Choosing a Consultant and Agreeing a Contract

At the heart of good consultancy is an effective contracting process. The process of arriving at a consultancy contract involves:

1) selecting a consultant to work with;
2) agreeing a contract with that consultant.

It is important to realise that the first 'selection' phase is an integral part of the overall contracting process and not something separate. When you are selecting a consultant you are contracting with that consultant. This chapter focuses on the selection phase, and Chapter 4 examines the contracting phase.

There is no right way of undertaking these two processes. The route you take will be affected by the size and nature of the consultancy work you want undertaken, your previous knowledge and experience of consultants, the timescales you are working to, your wish to involve different people in your organisation in the process, and your desire to attract the interest of a range of consultants and ensure equality of opportunity in the selection process. The result of the process should be a good match between your organisation and the consultant, a shared feeling that this is someone you can get on with, and the selection of someone who will 'deliver the goods'.

Long Routes and Short Routes

Figure 13 below summarises the steps you could use in a 'long' route and a 'short' route for selecting a consultant and agreeing a consultancy contract.

There are, of course, various 'middle' routes you could choose. For example, you could choose a consultant to work with on the basis of the exploratory meeting and their tender and not hold interviews.

The Long Route
1. Prepare a consultancy Brief and a consultant specification.
2. Identify consultants you might use.
3. Make initial contact with consultants.
4. Hold exploratory meeting with consultants.
5. Invite tenders from consultants.
6. Interview consultants.
7. Make a choice.
8. Hold a Contracting Meeting.
9. Agree a Contract.

The Short Route
1. Prepare a consultancy Brief and decide which consultant to use.
2. Make contact with the consultant.
3. Hold a combined exploratory and contracting meeting.
4. Agree a contract.

Figure 13: The Long Route and the Short Route for Selecting a Consultant and Agreeing a Contract

• The Long Route

Unlike staff selection procedures the consultant selection procedure is a negotiation. During the telephone conversations, exploratory meetings, preparation of written tenders and interviews with consultants that can make up a selection process, a process of negotiation is going on.

The consultant will be making an initial analysis of the problem you want to address. They will be assessing whether what you, the organisation, wants from the consultant, will achieve the outcomes you desire. They will be considering whether the consultancy process you have in mind has scope for tackling both the 'technical' problem and how you are dealing with that problem.

YOU **JOINT** **THE CONSULTANT**

FIRST PHASE : SELECTING A CONSULTANT

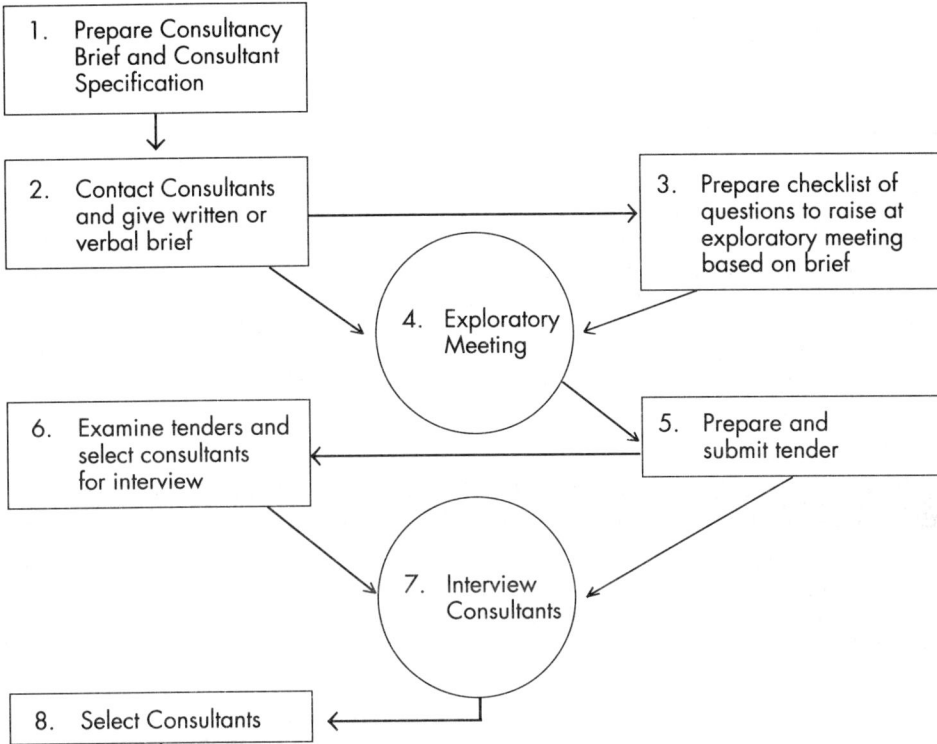

1. Prepare Consultancy Brief and Consultant Specification

2. Contact Consultants and give written or verbal brief

3. Prepare checklist of questions to raise at exploratory meeting based on brief

4. Exploratory Meeting

6. Examine tenders and select consultants for interview

5. Prepare and submit tender

7. Interview Consultants

8. Select Consultants

SECOND PHASE : AGREEING A CONTRACT

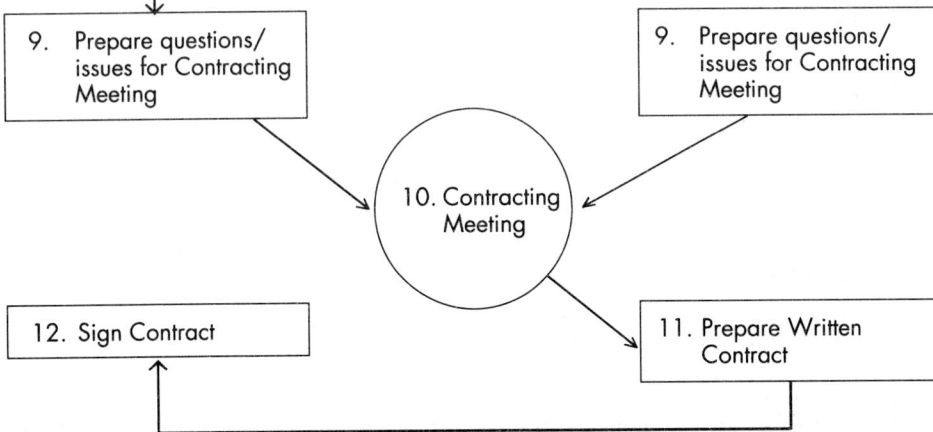

9. Prepare questions/ issues for Contracting Meeting

9. Prepare questions/ issues for Contracting Meeting

10. Contracting Meeting

12. Sign Contract

11. Prepare Written Contract

Figure 14: A Two-Way Contracting Process: the Long Route

The consultant will be making a judgement about whether the consultancy has a better than 50/50 chance of succeeding. They will try to influence the shape and nature of the consultancy to improve those odds, or not agree to proceed.

This two-way negotiation is illustrated in Figure 14. It shows how the 'long route' looks in a flow chart to both you, the organisation, and the consultant. Steps 1-8 in the flowchart are the key elements of the selection process. Steps 9–12 are the key elements in the contracting process (see next chapter).

● The Short Route

By contrast, Figure 15 is a flowchart of the short route. In effect, all the stages of selecting a consultant have been collapsed into two processes.

Firstly the organisation makes a decision about which consultant it wishes to approach on the basis of personal experience or recommendation, thereby removing the need for separate exploratory meetings, tenders and interviews. In this route you approach a consultant or team of consultants who you believe can carry out the consultancy task and who fit the consultant specification. Secondly there is a process of exploration between you, the organisation, and the consultant about the

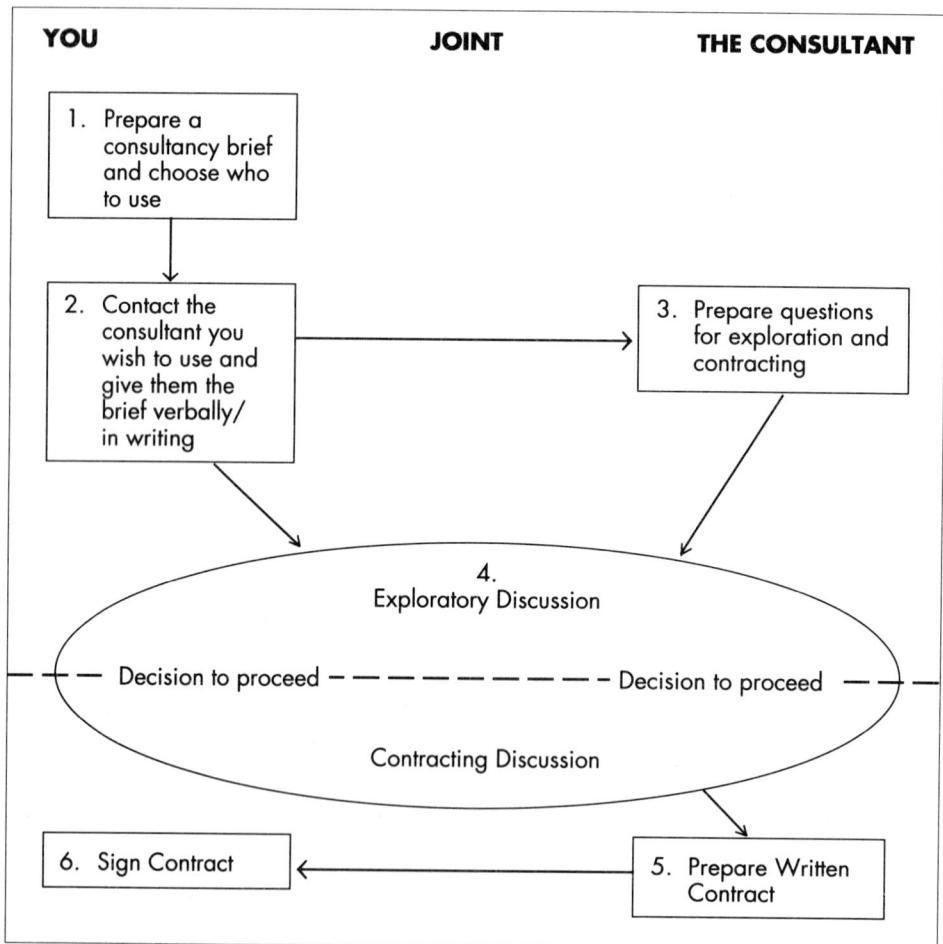

Figure 15:   A Two-Way Contracting Process: the Short Route

consultancy task which can either lead to a decision to proceed and hence agree a contract, or lead to a decision not to proceed.

The advantages of the different routes are:

The Long Route
- Ensures equality of opportunity in the process and allows for positive action.
- Allows comparisons of tenders from different consultants.
- Generates new ideas made by different consultants.
- Involves wider range of consultants.
- Ensures the choice does not reflect the personal contacts of one person in your agency.
- May feel more appropriate for a large consultancy task.

The Short Route
- Your or others' personal experience of the consultant is the basis of the selection part of the process.
- Allows for positive action in choosing a consultant.
- It is quicker.
- You may feel it is an appropriate use of resources for a small consultancy task.
- You will use someone you are confident will do the work well.

The Selection Process

Most organisations take the 'short route' to choosing a consultant although greater use is made of tenders and interviewing of consultants for larger pieces of work.

Each of the steps in the selection process for the 'long route' are now explored in detail, but most of these ideas also apply to meetings and conversations you have with consultants in the shorter route. If you choose to take a shorter route, then steps 3-6 will be of most relevance to you.

The steps are:

Step 1   Identify Consultants you might use
Step 2   Make Initial Contact with Consultants
Step 3   Hold Exploratory Meetings with Consultants
Step 4   Invite Tenders from Consultants
Step 5   Interview Consultants
Step 6   Make a Choice

● Step 1: Identify Consultants you might use

In order to choose a consultant you will need to have produced a consultancy brief and drawn up a consultant specification. This process is described in detail in the previous chapter.

There are four basic ways of identifying a consultant you might use. You may have already had personal contact with a consultant from previous work he has done with your organisation or even through social contacts. Alternatively you may have personal contact through someone in your organisation attending training courses run by that consultant. Where you have no previous contact or when you wish to invite interest from a wider range of as yet unknown consultants, you can either seek informal recommendations from another organisation or intermediary body, or use directories of consultants or advertise (see **Appendix 8**).

These four broad options for identifying consultants you could use are summed up in Figure 16.

When using any of these methods it will be important to make clear your consultant specification to attract suitable individuals or groups of consultants.

	Known To You	**Unknown To You**
Informal Contact	Consultants you have worked with previously or known socially	Consultants recommended by other organisations or intermediaries such as the Management Development Unit of the NCVO
Formal Contact	Consultants you know through contact at training courses or written material.	Advertise in the Press. Refer to directories of consultants.

Adapted from Reynolds (2)

Figure 16:   Ways of Identifying Consultants

In identifying consultants you could take positive action to encourage interest among consultants who experience unfair discrimination such as women, Black people and people with disabilities.

For example, your adverts could stress that you welcome applications from particular groups and you could specifically ask intermediaries and others to identify consultants from among these groups whom they would recommend.

In doing this you should not assume, for example, that women consultants are only interested in women issues or Black consultants on Black issues. Some consultants specialise in this way but this is not the same as taking positive action to attract interest among particular groups of consultants who experience discrimination and who offer a wide range of consultancy services.

● Step 2: Make Initial Contact with Consultants

Whether replying to people who have responded to your advert or writing to a selection of consultants drawn up by other means, your next step is to write or telephone the people concerned describing what you want. Experienced consultants will be used to dealing with an initial phone call or a letter of this kind. You should expect them to want to arrange a meeting with you before going into a detailed contracting process.

Questions to expect from Consultants on initial contact   The kind of questions *they* will want answered on the phone about an initial meeting are:

- What do you want to discuss?
- What is the general nature of the problem?
- Is there a written brief and can it be sent in advance?
- Who is the client for this consultancy?
- Who else will be at the meeting?
- Do you know that you want to begin a consultancy with me or is this an initial meeting that you are having with a number of consultants?
- What timescale is envisaged?

In some cases this telephone call could develop into what would normally take place at an exploratory meeting.

● Step 3: An Exploratory Meeting

This first meeting is exploratory and two-way. On the whole consultants will not expect to be paid a fee for this meeting but you might feel it fair to reimburse their travelling expenses. If you have taken the shorter route and already decided that the person you are meeting is the consultant you want to use, then this will at some stage become a contracting meeting as well.

Exploring The Problem   At an exploratory meeting the consultants you meet will want to explore your description of the problem, your diagnosis, what outcomes you want to achieve and what methods you want a consultant to use. They will want to go through your initial analysis using their knowledge and experience and be satisfied that it is a good starting point. The consultant will want to hear and will value your views but will also want to challenge your perceptions of the problem. You will get most out of this if you feel you have been heard by the consultant and are open to any new ideas or perceptions the consultant might bring at this early stage. To some extent meeting say three or four consultants in this way is getting some free consultancy analysis that may change your perceptions of the problem and alter the brief. It also provides you with some comparisons of the consultants and the qualities they bring. However, some consultants will be reluctant to come up with 'quick' solutions and may even feel resentful at you using them for 'free' consultancy in this way. The consultant, too, will be making their own initial judgements at this stage, particularly over your readiness for change and the potential she sees for working together in a collaboration.

General Approach   It is important to remember that consultants will inevitably have their own particular view of the world. Some may tend to see issues or problems as being rooted in organisational structures, systems or policies. Others will look for inter-personal conflict, group dynamics or power issues as the cause. And others may have a particular technique or approach that they will bring into your organisation to address the issues you identify. You need to assess whether the consultant's framework — the general approach and style they take — is relevant to your needs. Figure 17 gives suggestions as to questions you could ask.

Some questions you might consider asking at this stage are:

- What values underpin your approach to consultancy?

- What kind of approach do you take to dealing with problems or tasks of this kind?

- Describe examples of similar work you have undertaken and what elements were particularly important to their success.

Figure 17:   Questions to Ask Consultants at an Exploratory Meeting

Integrity and Trust   A less easily defined assessment you will need to make at the exploratory meeting is to what extent the consultants are behaving genuinely and with authenticity. Are they showing genuine interest in jointly exploring what your issues or concerns are, and their capacity to help you resolve them; or are they just trying to 'win' a contract or sell you a solution? Do you feel you can trust the consultant? Is this a person who might damage you, or who, as well as solving the 'technical' problem will be sensitive to you as people and as an organisation? It is possible that 'integrity' could be included in the consultant specification with the values you are looking for.

You should view the exploratory meeting, and any subsequent interviews and contracting processes, as a model of how the consultancy might work. Watching what the consultant does and how he behaves gives you direct information about his approach generally. Figure 18 is a list of indicators of consultant integrity and applies to interviews and contracting meetings. Essentially you are judging whether or not this is a person you get on with.

Some indicators as to whether the consultants you meet are behaving with integrity are:

- *The kinds of questions they ask.* Do they
  - ask what concerns you have about using a consultant?
  - ask direct questions about who you and others are?
  - ask questions about your expectations of them?
  - challenge and explore your assumptions?

- *The balance of their listening and speaking:*
  - do they ask open-ended, exploratory questions?
  - do they reflect on what you've said and relate it to their own experiences and knowledge?
  - are they jointly defining the problems and the plans?
  - do they appear to be 'selling' themselves or their 'product'?

- *The statements they make:*
  - Do they clearly and simply state their expectations of you?
  - Do they describe their capacity to undertake the work?
  - Do they say no directly to things you want but they can't provide?

- *The non-verbal communication:*
  - Do they show good inter-personal skills?
  - Do they show enthusiasm?

- *Their attention to the current conversation*
  - Do they reflect back their feelings about the current conversation?
  - Does it feel to you as though the distance between you and them is widening or closing?

Figure 18: Indicators of Consultant Integrity

● Step 4: Invite Tenders

Written tenders for a consultancy are the first stage in producing a written contract. Consultants produce them on the basis of any written material and brief you've provided and the issues raised on the telephone or at any exploratory meeting.

Two fictitious examples of tenders (both based on real consultancy contracts) are given in Appendices 1 and 2.

The first is a relatively long tender for a 60-day strategic review of a UK voluntary agency.

The second is a relatively short tender for a 3-day team review and development consultancy process for a small local voluntary agency.

The examples are not intended to be models of good practice in going about their respective consultancy tasks (although you might wish to use them as a basis for discussion of how to undertake a short team review or a substantial strategic review of an organisation). Rather they are included to illustrate how a consultancy task, be it small or big, requires a tender, and a subsequent contract that always covers certain areas.

When asking people to tender, you should state clearly what you want the tender to cover. You could send them a written guideline, as shown in Figure 19. If you wish the negotiation of the costs of the consultancy to be undertaken separately from negotiation of other aspects of the work, you can ask consultants to submit the budget element of the tender on an easily separated section from the main body of the tender.

● Step 5: Interviewing Consultants

You may wish to meet again some or all of the consultants who have submitted a

In writing your tender, please ensure you cover the following areas:

1. **The Purpose and Focus**
   The outcomes you will achieve, the specific areas of work, or issues you will include, and if necessary what is not included in the consultancy.

2. **Overall Approach**
   How you will approach the work in general terms, and the style you will adopt.

3. **Values, Motivation and Experience**
   A summary of why you want to do the consultancy, the knowledge, skills, experience and personal perspectives you bring, and your values.

4. **The Methodology**
   A reasonably detailed description of what you do and the roles you will play.

5. **The Product**
   The feedback you will give, oral or written, length and specification; general suggestions or specific action and so on. When that feedback will happen at different stages.

6. **Support and Involvement of the Organisation**
   The access you require to people and information in the organisation, and the tasks you expect people to carry out.

7. **Time Schedule**
   When the work will start, intermediate stages and completion dates.

8. **Roles, Accountability and Confidentiality**
   The roles that different people will play in the consultancy such as any advisory/ steering groups, and specific roles of any staff members; who you will be accountable to for the work; and the groundrules about who gets what information.

9. **Budget**
   Your fees and expenses for the work, and any additional 'hidden' time/money/ resources costs we might incur.

10. **The Consultants**
    Who will do the work, and if there is more than one person, how you will work together and who will be the lead contact person.

Figure 19: Tender Guidelines

tender. Most people are familiar with staff recruitment procedures but this may not be an appropriate form for interviewing consultants. These interviews are both a selection process *and* a contracting process in that the meeting will be a chance for:

- You to assess the suitability of the consultant(s).
- The consultants to assess you and your readiness to change.
- You and the consultant to explore the nature of the problems you want to address through using a consultant.

Remember you are recruiting someone to work with you to assist a process of change and not employing a member of staff. You will be using a consultant to help you go through a process of change in some way which is different from employing someone on a short-term contract to carry out a specific function or deliver a part of your service. The interview 'dynamics' will feel different as the relationship will be that of peer-peer rather than employer-employee, and will be more of a two-way process.

It is important that the consultants you interview are the ones that will be carrying out the work. Avoid interviewing a senior consultant, or consultancy group representative who then passes the work on to a junior to carry it out. This dilemma is discussed in more detail in the next chapter on the contracting process.

Who's Involved? An interview gives you the opportunity to involve others in your organisation in the process. The consultant may have met only one person during the exploratory meeting but an interview panel could include a wider range of people such as other staff, committee members or users. If the consultant is helping you to undertake a process of change, then ownership of that change process is more likely to happen if the people affected are involved in the selection process.

How will it be conducted?   You should decide in advance how you want to conduct the interviews:

- How long will the interview last — an hour?
- If the consultant has submitted a tender, will you invite them to make a brief 10–15 minute presentation at the start?
- Will you ask at the start whether the consultant minds being interrupted as they make their presentation or leave questions until the end?
- What key questions do you want to ask the consultant?
- How much do you want it to develop into a discussion rather than simply be the conventional question-and-answer format of staff recruitment interviews?
- How flexible will you be if the consultant wants to make it more of a discussion and ask you questions?
- Remember to end the interview with an explanation of when the consultant can expect to hear from you about your decision.

What to look out for   The presentation by the consultant, the way she responds to questions, and the questions she puts to you will all give important messages about whether they are the right person to do what you want. Consider during the presentation and the interview:

- Is the consultant's general approach or view of the world relevant to your needs?
- Is she showing genuine interest and behaving with integrity?
- How much emphasis is placed on values and are they what we want?
- How much genuine enthusiasm and energy for the task and our organisation is being demonstrated?
- How would it feel if this were a presentation of some feedback during the consultancy?
- Am I feeling empowered by what I'm receiving?
- How will others in the organisation respond to this person?
- Is their both sufficient rigour and sufficient flexibility in their methods?
- Is what she is proposing open to further negotiation at a contracting meeting – for example, on the methodology, allocation of time, or the costs?
- Does she have the resources to carry out the task – personal and administrative? Will she deliver?

• Step 6: Make a Choice

Your starting point for making a choice is your initial consultancy brief and the consultant specification you drew up. The information you have gathered to help you make a choice includes:

- Personal contact through the exploratory meeting and the interview.
- Written material in the form of a written tender.

Personal Contact   The exploratory meeting and the interview will have given you insights into the general approach or view of the world that the consultants have — and whether this is the approach of most relevance to you. You will have gained an appreciation of how authentic they are from the exploratory meetings and interviews. You should know whether they are genuinely interested in jointly exploring your issues and concerns. And the way the meetings went will have been a model of how the consultancy itself might work in terms of:

- the questions asked;
- the balance of listening and speaking;
- the statements made;
- the non–verbal communication.

You will also have gained an appreciation of their capacity to carry out the task including the necessary administrative back-up if it is a large piece of work.

The consultant specification provides the basis for assessing whether the consultants have the personal attributes you want. It is worth repeating that unless the consultant(s) have the values and skills you require, there is less likelihood of establishing the kind of consultancy relationship you want.

Written Information   The written tender should be assessed against the initial consultancy brief, the tender guidelines and any review of that brief arising from exploratory meetings with the consultant. The consultant may have deliberately departed from the brief because they have a different analysis or perspective about the problem you wish to address and how it should be carried out. This should not be grounds for rejecting the tender. Each tender should be assessed on its merit. Unlike the process of assessing tenders for compliance with a detailed service contract specification, a consultancy tender represents another part of the contracting process. It is part of the process of you and a consultant reaching agreement about ways of working together on the key problems you want to resolve.

Some broad questions that may help in assessing written tenders are:

- Will it fulfil the objectives or terms of reference?
- Does the overall approach seem appropriate to our organisation?
- Does it show an understanding of the kind of organisation we are?
- Are the values explicit and are they what we want?
- Does the detailed methodology seem right?
- Will the process create ownership, help us to feel empowered and avoid dependency?
- Are the tasks achievable in the time allocated?
- Is there potential for flexibility?
- Is the timescale what we want?
- Is the budget within the limits we set? If it is not, does it rule the tender out or does there appear to be scope for amending the work and the costs involved and still achieve the brief?
- Are roles clearly spelt out?
- Are lines of accountability and groundrules on confidentiality clear?
- Does it demonstrate enthusiasm and energy for the task and our organisation?
- Is the 'product' clearly described?
- Are the consultant's expectations of you clearly spelt out?
- Is it clear who will do the work and is this the person(s) you want?

It is unlikely that any tender will answer all these questions completely to your satisfaction. So you will need to make an overall judgement about which has the best fit and the extent to which the proposals are renegotiable.

Judging tenders by their costs is made easier if you have given a budget in the initial consultancy brief. You can, for example, compare the fees quoted and how they are calculated. Appendices 2 and 3 give examples of how costs were put into tenders for a large strategic review and a shorter team building process. Some consultants will quote a daily rate plus expenses and arrive at a total cost for the work. Others will give a fixed fee that they have calculated – often on the basis of a daily rate but taking into account other costs. There is no hard and fast rule about fees and methods used by consultants for agreeing payment:

" The professional bodies representing consultants offer a range of advice and standards of professional behaviour for agreeing payment for consultancy work. One regards it as 'unprofessional conduct' to agree payment 'on any basis other than a fixed fee agreed in advance'; another says only that fees will be based on service provided for the specific task being carried out . . . .

The Institute of Management Consultants (9) offer the following guidance:

there must be a clear understanding between client and consultant

- about the objective of the assignment
- the fees or the basis of the fees to be charged.

So in addition to defining appropriate terms of reference, a consultant's proposal should quote

- a fixed fee
- a range within which the fee will fall or the fee rate(s) to be charged in terms of time (hour, day, week) or other defined basis. " (6)

The question of time and money will be a subject for further discussion between you and the consultant at the contracting meeting (see Chapter 4).

References   A common element in staff recruitment is to ask for references. But it is not certain how valuable these are as they often contain only general comments and tend to leave out negative criticisms. These problems are compounded in the case of consultants' references by the issue of confidentiality.

Most consultants view their work with organisations as confidential and in some cases will be unwilling even to reveal who they work with. If consultants do give you names of people and organisations with whom they have worked, it is only human nature for them to put you in contact with organisations with whom they know they worked well, or who liked them (not necessarily the same thing).

It is also the case that the problems your organisation is experiencing, the outcomes you want and the nature of the people involved are completely different. You will not know whether the experience referred to is appropriate or not.

References then may have only very limited use to confirm that consultants are who they say they are, and have done what they say they have done.

An alternative to a reference is to ask the organisation quoted as a referee to send examples of any written reports the consultant produced for them. Such material will give you some idea of the quality of writing and presentation that you can expect from the consultant.

Payment   It costs a consultant money to go through the process of attending exploratory meetings, writing submissions, attending interviews and agreeing contracts. Very often this is unpaid time and if it fails to produce any work is very expensive.

As a result you could view this as the consultant's problem to resolve and indeed many do simply increase their fees for all contracts to recoup the cost of their time and travel when seeking new work.

Alternatively you could offer to pay consultants' travelling expenses (as you would in recruiting staff) and make a payment in contribution to the time they have spent in preparing tenders and so on (from which you may benefit when agreeing a final contract with the consultant you have chosen).

CHOOSING A CONSULTANT
KEY POINTS

1. At the heart of a good consultancy is an effective contracting process involving:

    1) Selecting a consultant to work with
    2) Agreeing a contract with that consultant

2. The selection process is an integral part of the overall contracting process and not something separate. When you are selecting a consultant, you are also contracting with that consultant.

3. There are long routes and short routes for selecting a consultant and agreeing a contract. The route you take will be affected by the size and nature of the consultancy work you want undertaken, your previous knowledge and experience of consultants, the timescales, the involvement of others in the organisation, the range of consultants you want to attract and ensuring equality of opportunity.

4. The steps in the long route for selecting a consultant are:

    Step 1.   Identify consultants you might use
    Step 2.   Make initial contact with consultants
    Step 3.   Hold exploratory meetings with consultants
    Step 4.   Invite tenders from consultants
    Step 5.   Interview consultants
    Step 6.   Make a choice

    If you choose a shorter route, then steps 3–6 will be of most relevance to you.

5. The selection process is a two-way discussion in which you are assessing the consultants you meet and they are assessing the potential for working together and your readiness to change. Both you and the consultant are judging whether or not you can get on with each other.

6. You should view the selection and contracting processes — meetings, correspondence and so on — as a model of how the consultancy might work. The consultant's behaviour in this process gives you direct information about how they work generally.

7. In assessing consultants you need to be sure that their general approach and style is what you want and that they are behaving authentically and with integrity.

8. If you ask for tenders, you should send consultant's guidelines for producing them to ensure you receive the information you want to help you make a choice. Consultancy tenders should be viewed as a part of the contracting process and negotiable. You must judge each tender on its merits and decide which has the best 'fit' and what you want to renegotiate.

Chapter four

Agreeing a Contract

Process And Administration Contracts

The Process Contract
- Level of Detail
- Evaluation

The Administration Contract
- Costs and Payments
- Payment

The Contracting Meeting
- Preparation
- The Consultant's Agenda
- Your Agenda
- Review how the Meeting is Going
- Who's Involved
- The 'Lead' Consultant

Two-Stage Contracts

Treat Your Consultants Well

Process And Administration Contracts

You have chosen the consultant with whom you want to work. The next task is to agree a contract.

A contract is an explicit agreement of what you and the consultant expect from each other and how you are going to work together. To assist you and the consultant achieve this:

- you may already have produced a written brief;
- they may have produced a tender and other ideas may have been raised during exploratory meetings and interviews.

But if you have used the 'short' route to choosing a consultant, your contracting meeting will include greater elements of exploration and questioning .

It may be useful to divide contracts in two:

1. **The Process contract** which describes the purpose of the consultancy, the overall approach, the methodology, the product and feedback, the support and involvement of the organisation, time schedules, roles, accountability and confidentiality.

2. **The administration contract** which deals with issues of time, money, expenses, payments, cancellation clauses, the people and accountability.

The Process Contract

The process contract is the description of what you and the consultant expect from each other and how you are going to work together. It has similar headings to that provided in the tender guidelines but in drawing up the process contract you and the consultant can add all the ideas and suggestions that have been generated during the exploratory meetings, tender submissions and interviews. For example, you may wish to put forward aspects of ways of working proposed by other consultants who submitted tenders.

Figure 20 lists the key headings that should be discussed and agreed at the contract meeting about the process of the consultancy.

● Level Of Detail

The level of detail about the problems to be addressed and the methods to be used is likely to vary according to the nature of the contract. For example, in a team-building consultancy the diagnosis of the problems within the team and how to resolve them can be a sensitive and difficult task. The specific methods such as self-analysis questionnaires, team sculpts and so on may be described in general terms. But these may be the first tasks to be undertaken in the contract — not something to be done during the contracting meeting. If you press a consultant to say exactly what they will do and how in these circumstances they may interpret this as resistance or manipulation by you. This may lead to further discussion about the purpose of the consultancy, the general approach and the desire to proceed.

By contrast in planning a strategic review of your organisation the consultant may want to discuss specific methods in considerable detail. Appendix 2 is an example of a detailed tender that formed the basis of a contract for undertaking a strategic review. It may not always be necessary to ask the consultant to replicate the tender details in the contract. It may be sufficient to receive written confirmation that refers to the tender and adds any amendments made at the contracting meeting.

There is a balance to be reached in the contracting meeting between agreeing sufficient detail to be clear about what is going to happen, who will be involved,

1. **The Purpose and Focus**
   A statement of what the consultancy will achieve, the specific areas of work or issues included and if necessary what is specifically excluded.
2. **Overall Approach**
   The general approach to the work and the style to be adopted.
3. **The Methodology**
   A reasonably detailed description of what will be done and the roles to be played by the consultant.
4. **The Product**
   The feedback to be given – oral or written; its length and level of detail – general suggestions or specific action; how regularly it will be provided.
5. **Support and Involvement of the Organisation**
   Access the consultant requires to people and information in the organisation. Tasks that people in the organisation are expected to carry out.
6. **Time Schedule**
   When the work will start, intermediate stages and completion dates.
7. **Roles, Accountability and Confidentiality**
   - Roles to be played by any advisory/reference or steering group and specific roles of any staff members.
   - The individual or person to whom the consultant is accountable.
8. **Evaluation**
   - The mechanism for reviewing and, if necessary, amending the work as it proceeds.
   - The method for evaluating the process and outcomes of the consultancy once the work has been completed.
   - The groundrules about what information is kept confidential to the consultant and who gets what information and feedback from the consultant .
9. **The Consultants**
   Who will do the work, and if more than one person, who the lead person is and how they will work together.

Figure 20:   The Process Contract

and when; yet leaving sufficient room for the consultant to make judgements and choices about the problems and how to tackle them as the consultancy proceeds.

● Evaluation

Evaluation of the consultancy needs to be built in from the start, both as the work proceeds in order to change things as you go along — formative evaluation; and at the end when the work is completed. Chapter 7 describes what to evaluate and how in more detail but it is crucial to include in the contract a way of reviewing how the consultancy is going whilst it is happening. It is of little use to the consultant to leave it to the end to tell them you are dissatisfied as they cannot do anything to change it. And the consultant may want to make changes to the contract as a result of what she finds. Discussions of how the consultancy is going is a feature of good consultancy practice, so expect to do it and have it written in the contract.

The Administration Contract

The administration contract is relatively easy to compile once the more difficult process contract has been agreed (see Figure 21 below). It protects both you and the consultant. Confusion over such factors can cause resentment or anger which interrupts the more important dilemmas about the consultancy task.

Agreeing the administration contract is a key part of the contracting process, but

1. The Organisation
2. The Person Involved
3. An Outline Of The Work
4. The Key Dates and Timescales
5. Fees to be paid – per day and in total
6. Expenses to be covered:
    - travel
    - subsistence – meals and accommodation
    - administration costs
7. Individual or group to whom the consultant reports
8. Form and schedule of payment
    - eg. by cheque at end of each month in which the work takes place, according to time
9. VAT
    An additional topic that could be included is copyright and use of written materials or reports.

Figure 21: The Administration Contract

if you prefer it can be a matter for the consultant and the lead person within your organisation rather than a whole staff team or reference group who may have been involved in agreeing the process contract.

● Costs and Payments

Your initial consultancy brief should have indicated the budget and timescales of the contract. And whilst choosing the consultant you may have had further discussion about the costs and timing of the work. But a key part of the contracting process is to reach final agreement on how much the consultant will do, what fees and expenses they will be paid and the method and schedule of payment.

When agreeing costs, remember to cover the headings below in your discussion if only to agree that no costs will be charged for certain items

- **Fees** (eg. total fee or per day rate and total)
    eg. Preparation Fees
    Delivery Fee
    Follow-up Fee
- **Travelling Expenses**
    - car mileage rate (eg. 41p per mile)
    - rail fares (eg. 2nd class)
    - bus fares
    - air fares
    - use of taxis
- **Subsistence Expenses**
    - maximum daily allowance for meals and accommodation
- **Administration Costs**
    - typing
    - postage
    - photocopying (eg. 6p per copy)
    - printing
    - materials (eg. paper, pens etc.)
- **V.A.T.**
    - the rate
    - items to which it applies
      (eg. VAT at the rate prevailing on the day of invoice is chargeable on all costs).

You will need to be clear what additional financial costs you may need to pay over-and-above what you are paying the consultant – for example, staff travel costs, room hire and so on.

• Payment

Two common payment methods include:

- Payment for work done on receipt of invoice.
  - either at the end of all the work, or for work done during each month.
- Initial, interim and final instalments up to an agreed limit over a period of time. And, for example, payment of the final instalment could be subject to receiving a final report.

The Contracting Meeting

• Preparation

The consultant is likely to take any tender they have submitted as the starting point for the discussion. And you need to prepare a list of questions, issues and suggestions to raise at that meeting. Both you and the consultant should agree in advance (perhaps over the phone) how you want to handle the meeting:

- Who will be there
- How the meeting will run
  - will the consultant chair it?
- What the meeting will cover
- The length of the meeting
- Facilities needed
  - flipcharts
  - diaries
  - OHP
- Expectations about the level of detail at the outcome of the meeting.

On one level the contracting meeting is about agreeing the 'mechanics' of the consultancy — who will do what, when and how: the process contract .

But the contracting meeting will also be a part of the diagnostic phase of the consultancy. There will be a lot more going on than sorting out the nuts and bolts.

• The Consultant's Agenda

The consultant will be trying to:

- Analyse what is going on in your organisation both to ensure the contract will achieve its purpose and to understand your organisation better before the work begins.
- Understand further the "politics" of the organisation and where there might be resistance to change.
- Use the contracting meeting as an intervention to 'model':
  - establishing rapport between them and you.
  - establishing a collaborative way of working.
  - building mutual trust and confidence.

• Your Agenda

You will be using the contracting meeting to:

- Inform the consultant as fully as possible about the issues and concerns you want to be addressed. Do not hold back (or allow others to hold back) information you know to be relevant and important. It is easy to sabotage a consultancy by allowing a contract to be agreed and then during the process introduce new information that negates the original agreement.

- Agree a timescale and time allocation that is right for you and achievable by the consultant. Avoid a natural tendency to cut the timescale and time allocation down to the bare minimum. Whilst you might have immediate problems and issues to deal with that make the time given to the consultancy seem a luxury, it is false economy to be overly restrictive. Make sure that during the contracting discussion you give work on the consultancy a priority and plan ways of creating space in the workloads of the relevant people to enable them to be involved, to have the time to consider change, and to act on the outcomes.
- Arrive at a timescale that meets your needs and those of the consultant and be specific about deadlines.
- Understand the consultant(s) better — their potential strengths and weaknesses and their way of working.

● Review How The Meeting Is Going

During the contracting meeting it will be useful for you and the consultant to check out how the meeting is going. This should be an explicit discussion to ensure that you and the consultant are happy with the nature of the process and the outcome. An authentic consultant will do this without prompting.

If there are serious difficulties in the way the meeting is going, it might be useful to bear in mind some groundrules about contracting:

- Responsibility for the relationship is two-way.
  You and the consultant are equally responsible for making things work.
- The contract is entered into freely.
- You can say 'no' to the consultant. And the consultant can say 'no' to you.
- Make sure the consultant agrees to a written contract. Ask them to write it for you as it's what they're used to doing.
- If you want to change the contract at this stage, tell the consultants. They can cope with change; they can't cope if you don't let them know about it.
- Don't ask the consultant for something they can't do or don't have.
- You may end up with no contract at the end of the meeting. Don't worry. There are other consultants.

● Who's Involved In The Contracting Meeting:

Your Organisation   Depending upon the nature of the consultancy task, the people at the contracting meeting from your organisation could be:

- All the people with whom the consultant will be working eg. for a team-building process the consultant might meet the whole team.
- A group of people representing different groups with whom the consultant will be working
  eg. for the development of a staff development policy, representatives of the management team, different departments, support staff, a black workers' support group and the trade union.
- A reference group that have been involved right from the start in drawing up the brief and selecting the consultant and who will continue to provide a point of reference for the consultant during the work.
  eg. a reference group of staff, committee members and users was established for a strategic review of the department of a UK-wide voluntary agency that had a mix of people with different personal perspectives.

It is essential that the right people are in the room to draw up the contract. The consultant will want to be clear about exactly who the client is (as distinct from advisory groups etc.) and that they contract with them direct. This is particularly important for large or complex organisations where the consultancy task affects people in different departments.

The Consultants It is also crucial that the consultants at the contracting meeting are those that will be doing the consultancy task. Avoid holding a contracting meeting with only the manager of the consultant involved. Complex 3 or 4-way relationships can be created as described earlier in the use of internal consultants (Chapter 1). At worst you could be in the position of your manager agreeing a contract with the consultant's manager with neither you nor the consultant present, as illustrated below:

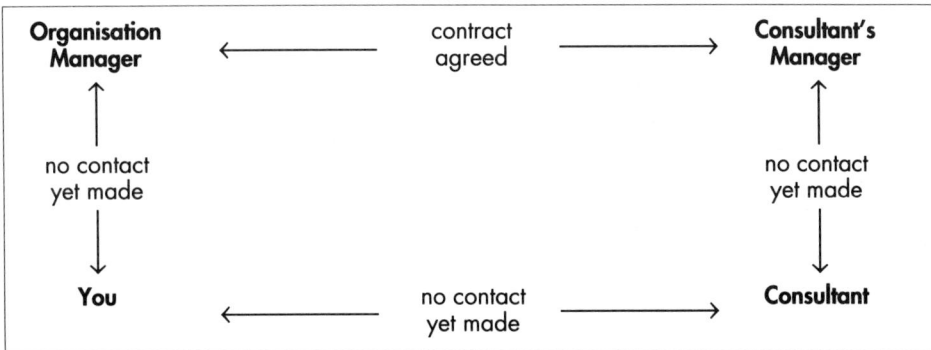

Organisation Manager	← contract agreed →	**Consultant's Manager**
↑ no contact yet made ↓		↑ no contact yet made ↓
You	← no contact yet made →	**Consultant**

In effect a consultancy contract has been agreed between two managers yet neither of the actual participants has given a commitment to begin or to work together. Inevitably when this happens you and the consultant eventually do meet and have to renegotiate and agree a new and possibly different contract.

To avoid this either hold a meeting where *all* the people in the relationship are present, or proceed from the bottom up, a process illustrated in Figure 22.

● The 'Lead' Consultant

When using a team of consultants be sure that one person clearly has the role of 'lead' consultant and is accountable for the consultancy contract. This helps to ensure clear channels for communication and, if needed, negotiation between you and the consultants. The consultants may not operate as a hierarchy — many don't — but functionally you should expect one person in that team to be responsible for the conduct of the work.

Two-Stage Contracts

A two-stage contract can allow the organisation and the consultant time to get to know each other better and to confirm that there are shared perceptions.

The first stage in this approach is a short contract which involves clarifying the problems, your organisation getting familiar with the consultant, and the consultant getting a greater understanding of you. This could take two or three days or be a substantial separate 'diagnosis' contract in its own right. At the end of the agreed period there is a review meeting. If either you or the consultant are dissatisfied with

(1)

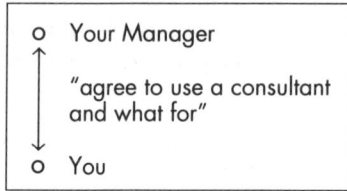

(2)

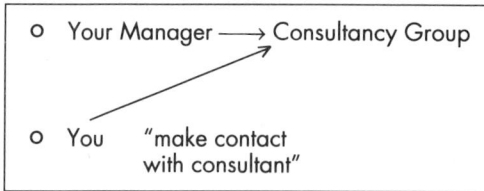

(3)

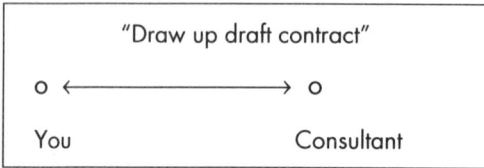

(4)

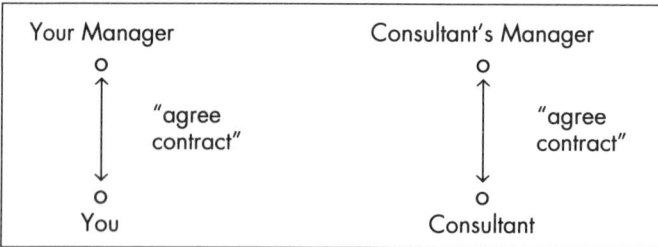

(5)

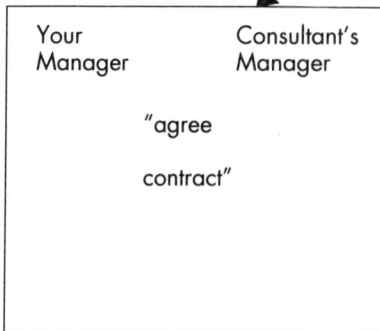

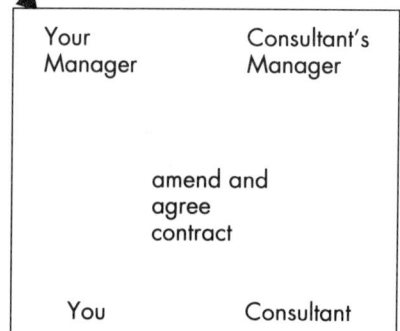

Figure 22: A 4-way Contracting Process

the other or feel there are significant differences in perception about the problem to be addressed, then you agree not to proceed.

If you agree to proceed then you move on to the second stage. This would be an agreement on the work to be carried out, the outcomes desired and the time to be spent.

The advantages of this process are two-fold. There is time made available to have a thorough look at the nature of the problem rather than feel there is pressure to rush into action. And neither side finds themselves in what could be a long-term, financially heavy commitment with which they are unhappy. It also gives you the opportunity to use different consultants for different aspects of the work or tasks to be achieved. For example, if the diagnosis is that you need a new fundraising strategy, you could identify specialist consultants to help you with that.

One disadvantage is that if the consultants are being honest and clear in raising your awareness of some unpalatable messages about your organisation, then you could use this two-stage approach as a means of dismissing the consultant and avoiding the issues or resisting changes that are needed.

The consultant's diagnosis of internal conflict simply becomes a political football between those people in the conflict — the separation of the diagnosis from the action phases disempowers the consultant from giving you support in managing the issues they have identified.

The first example below illustrates how this approach was used with a group of small voluntary organisations and the second how it worked in a more substantial review of the structure of a large voluntary organisation.

A TWO-STAGE CONTRACT

A consultant worked with three different small voluntary youthwork organisations to assist each one to create a staff development policy and practice relevant to their needs. Each organisation had 8 days' consultancy time and this was divided up into two stages:

STAGE	PHASE	LENGTH
1st Stage	I. Negotiating the initial contract including who the consultant is, confidentiality, style, commitment, focus of the work.	
	II. Investigating the issues within the organisations that may form the focus for the consultancy through interviews, attending meetings, reading and so on.	2 days approx.
	III. Renegotiating a final contract for the consultancy work.	
2nd Stage	IV. Assisting staff to develop and test different approaches to the work.	5 days
	V. Attending meetings with staff to discuss issues and action within the organisation.	
	VI. Drawing out the staff development policy implications for their organisation	1 day
		TOTAL: 8 DAYS

ANOTHER TWO-STAGE CONTRACT

A large UK-based voluntary organisation working in different countries used a two-stage contract to look at their structure and organisation.

The first stage was a diagnostic phase in which the consultants were asked to assist the organisation to identify the strengths and weaknesses of its current structure.

At the end of this stage the organisation was in a position to make choices:

- to judge that no substantial change was necessary and not to proceed with any further stages;
- to widen the information collection and diagnosis further using the same or different consultants — or no consultant at all;
- to move into the next phase of planning possible new structures for discussion and agreement with or without the consultants; and with the wider involvement of others in the organisation.

Treat Your Consultants Well

A contract is a two-way agreement. It places obligations on the consultant and it places obligations on you. Some aspects of this will be written into the contract, such as the amount, form and schedule of payment; or the information you will make available to the consultant and the tasks you will carry out.

Other aspects may be unwritten and amount to no more than good manners. Treating consultants as 'extras' on your organisational stage is as unhelpful as putting them in a starring role. If you have booked an appointment with a consultant, keep it, or at least give plenty of notice to rearrange it. Respect them as people with feelings and emotions. Don't treat them as though you are doing them a favour. Respect their boundaries and values. Avoid scapegoating them for your problems.

Be open and honest with them if you are not satisfied with what they are doing and take their views and judgements in good faith unless you have proven grounds for thinking otherwise.

AGREEING A CONTRACT
KEY POINTS

1. A contract is an explicit agreement of what you and the consultant expect from each other and how you are going to work together.

2. Contracts can be divided into:
    A Process Contract that describes the purpose of the consultancy, the overall approach, the methodology, the product and feedback, the support and involvement of the organisation, time schedules, roles, accountability and confidentiality.
    An Administration Contract that deals with issues of time, money, expenses, payments, cancellation clauses, the people and accountability.

3. The level of detail about the problems to be addressed and consultancy methods to be used will vary according to the nature of the contract. There is a balance to be reached in agreeing sufficient detail to be clear and agree about what is going to happen, who will be involved and when; yet leaving sufficient room for the consultant to make judgements and choices about the problems and how to tackle them as the consultancy proceeds.

4. The contract should be clear about what information is confidential to the consultant and unattributable, and who will have access to the consultant's feedback/report. It should be clear that the confidentiality agreement does not extend to illegal or seriously damaging practice that should be reported in an attributable way within your organisation.

5. A process for evaluating and amending the consultancy as it proceeds (formative evaluation) and at the end (summative evaluation) should be built into the contract.

6. You should review how the contracting meeting is going during the meeting.

7. You need to be clear about who should be at the contracting meeting from your organisation in order to draw up the contract and ensure ownership of what is agreed.

8. The consultant will want to be clear about exactly who the client is (as distinct from advisory groups etc.) and that they contract with them direct.

9. Make sure that the consultants at the contracting meeting are those that will be doing the consultancy task.

10. Two-stage contracts can be agreed in which the first stage is primarily about familiarisation and diagnosis of the problem or issue. The second 'implementation' stage is dependent upon a review at the end of the first stage, thus giving you the option of not proceeding unless you are happy to do so, or of choosing a different, perhaps specialist, consultant to carry out the second stage.

11. A contract is a two-way agreement that places obligations on both you and the consultant. There will be agreements in writing about what you are to do as part of the consultancy and there are unwritten understandings that amount to no more than good manners in the way you treat the consultants you work with.

Chapter five

Diagnosis and Information Gathering

What is Diagnosis?

Diagnosis is the process of understanding and describing the issue or problem you want to address.

As a result of the diagnosis you should be clear about the problem requiring a solution, have identified the forces that are causing it to exist and have the basis for choosing an effective way of bringing about change to resolve the problem.

Crucially the purpose of diagnosis is to generate insight, understanding and a motivation for action about a problem. Diagnosis in a consultancy is *not* the same as research. The difference is summed up in Figure 23.

This distinction between research and consultancy does not mean that consultants are in any way less professional. Rather that the choice of information gathered, the way it is collected, the timescales and the cost of a consultancy diagnosis process are designed to lead to action and to reflect a concern for the attitudes of the organisation towards the outcome. In particular there is an overt recognition that the diagnosis of the problem involves someone — you and/or the consultant — making a judgement about the problem and what to do about it.

Steps In The Diagnostic Process

The basic steps that you and the consultant will take in carrying out a diagnosis will be:

Step 1. **Identifying The Presenting Problem**
This is the problem as you *see* it in the organisation.
Step 2. **Choosing A Limited Number of Areas To Be Examined**
Deciding what particular questions you want answered on the 'technical' problem.
Step 3. **Deciding Who Will Be Involved**
This is both deciding who will take part in the consultancy process and the roles they will play.
Step 4. **Choosing How The Information Will Be Collected**
- Interview — individually or in groups
- Group Activities
- Questionnaires
- Diagnostic Tools
- Document Analysis
- Observation
Step 5. **Collecting The Information**
Step 6. **Funnelling, Summarising and Analysing The Information**
This is the key part of the process including:
- focusing on the important pieces of information
- drawing together the key points
- analysing what it means and its implications

Starting Points

● Your Starting Point

You may have done a lot of diagnosis and information gathering about the problem you want to tackle during the process of deciding what you want to use a consultant for, selecting a consultant and agreeing a contract.

If you took the shorter route through this procedure you may have spent only a limited amount of time exploring the problem you want to address and gathering relevant views, opinions and factual information. You may have done little or no

The purpose of diagnosis in consultancy is to create action, not just generate understanding.

Research Approach	**Action Approach**
The researcher:	The consultant:
Is interested in all factors that impact the problem at hand	is interested in factors which are under the control of the client and affect the problem
Regards being comprehensive and complete in the diagnosis as essential	Regards completeness and comprehensiveness as unnecessary. It can be overwhelming at the point of deciding what to do.
Can do research on their own. The organisation doesn't have to be involved as part of the research team.	Regards the client's involvement in the study as important at each stage.
Tries to eliminate their own bias and intuition. A heavy emphasis is placed on objectivity and hard data.	Is paid for their bias and intuition — it is called judgement. They use all the feelings and perceptions they have in addition to hard data.
Is essentially neutral toward whether the organisation approves of the outcomes of the study.	Is deeply concerned about the attitude of the client toward the outcome of the study.

Adapted from Peter Block (5)

Figure 23:   The Purpose of Diagnosis

diagnosis of the problem you want to address at the outset. Your contract may include working with the consultant to undertake the diagnosis as an explicit first phase. The consultancy contract may even be solely about doing a diagnosis — perhaps as part of an explicit two-stage contract in which consultancy support during the planning and implementation phases of change is negotiated at the end of the initial first diagnostic phase (see Chapter 4).

● The Consultant's Starting Point

Whatever you may have done by way of diagnosis, the consultant will want to continue to explore deeper and deeper layers of the problems you want to tackle. That's her job.

A consultant will not be content with the problem you present as the real problem without doing their own diagnosis and analysis. This is not because consultants think you are bound to have got the diagnosis wrong. Rather the consultant will want to be sure that your preconceived ideas about the issues are tested out and that you and he arrive at a shared analysis. There may well be sectional interests within your organisation who are in dispute about the problem or have different perceptions of need. The consultant will want to identify what these are.

You should be wary of consultants who accept unquestioningly the problem you present as the basis for planning and implementing change. And you should question your own motives if you expect consultants to do so. Such an agreeable style of consultancy may prevent the consultant from rocking the boat but is unlikely to move you beyond what you would have done anyway.

Some diagnosis by the consultant may have occurred during the contracting process, but the time limits and constraints inherent in agreeing a contract will mean a consultant will want to spend more time diagnosing the problems at the start. Depending on the nature of the consultancy task and the relationship you have created, you and they will continue to be diagnosing what is happening, why, and what to do about it throughout the contract.

Who Does the Diagnosis?

The consultant's primary concern is to get both a good diagnosis of the problem *and* to ensure *you* own it. Consultants know that they can use the most advanced consultancy tools for analysing a problem in your organisation but unless you are willing to act on that analysis it is wasted work.

There are three basic approaches to making use of the consultant's diagnostic skills and methods: self-diagnosis in which the consultant facilitates you to undertake your own diagnosis; joint diagnosis in which you and the consultant both contribute a diagnosis of the problem; and independent diagnosis in which the consultant does the diagnosis and gives you the results.

● Self-diagnosis

The consultant can act as a facilitator to you undertaking your own diagnosis. She can assist you to carry out the interviews, discussions and fact finding and provide you with techniques to analyse the results. In this approach you will ensure greatest ownership of the outcome. But it runs the greatest risk of being a self-fulfilling process because you may not be fully challenged about your preconceived ideas, or not take full account of experiences and knowledge outside your organisation.

● Joint diagnosis

A collaborative approach to diagnosis involves you and the consultant collecting information, jointly analysing the problems and both contributing suggestions for change. This gives you the benefit of the consultant's knowledge and experience about the issues or problems and requires the consultant to have techniques for helping you to undertake this process yourself.

This approach combines the two roles at opposite ends of the consultancy spectrum — process facilitator and policy advocate. As such it is hardest to make work. You and the consultant may disagree, for example, about the analysis. In these circumstances you need to be clear about who has final say on what is written or recommended, or whether two reports are produced describing the different viewpoints. It requires careful negotiation at the outset and constant attention when under way both to the problem being addressed and to your relationship with the consultant.

● Independent diagnosis

A wholly independent diagnosis hands over to the consultant the task of gathering information, making an analysis and suggesting solutions. This places greatest emphasis on the importance of a consultant's technical expertise on the problem, but runs the greatest risk of you rejecting it as your ownership of the consultant's findings will be at its lowest. Even if you completely trust the consultant, you may still not be prepared to take the action they recommend if it is very disagreeable to you. The consultant will need to take you through their information, analysis and recommendations in a way that ensures you develop ownership of it. In particular the consultant will want to avoid a situation where their feedback about how to resolve conflicts in your organisation being just another item for people to have conflict about.

Self-Diagnosis	The consultant facilitated a working group of staff and managers in an agency to draw up a staff development policy. The members of the group were helped to draw up a definition of staff development for their agency and agree a description of what was already happening in the agency that could be described as staff development processes, and the group were then helped to plan a process of gathering information from other agencies about their staff development policies and from their colleagues about what processes of staff development needed to be changed or added. This information and feedback was used by the group to agree their 'diagnosis' and to plan new staff development policy and procedures and how they could be implemented.
Joint Diagnosis	The consultant chaired the working group on staff development and in that role also offered personal knowledge and experience about staff development in general and specific problems in the agency. The consultant helped to gather information about staff development by doing some of the interviewing of a cross-section of the staff. During the discussion and diagnosis he actively contributed to the suggestions for the possible content of the new staff development policy.
Independent Diagnosis	The consultant met staff in the different departments to find out what staff development processes were already in place and what changes people wanted to see. Using this information and his knowledge and experience of staff development policy and practice in other organisations, the consultant presented a paper to a working party describing the current situation (his diagnosis) and making recommendations for change.

Figure 24:   Three approaches to diagnosis

Figure 24 illustrates what these three approaches look like in practice for a consultancy to assist an organisation to create a staff development policy.

Diagnosing how you are dealing with the Problem

During the diagnostic process you and the consultant need to focus on issues to do with both the technical problem on which you are working (management structure, fundraising strategies, practice development and so on) and how the problem is being dealt with (working relationships, management style, where power is located and how it is used, attitudes to social equality and so on).

Whilst gathering and analysing information about the technical problem you should reflect on your own behaviour and that of others in the organisation. What does this tell you about the changes needed in how the organisation is run in order to implement the 'technical' solutions to the problem?

When the consultant was interviewing a middle manager about the management structure, he realised that the answers were all geared towards ensuring that the person moved away from being line managed by one of the regional directors.

The issue here was not necessarily to do with structure but was to do with management style and a conflict of values.

Specifically, it was to do with the values of the middle manager being interviewed and the way he responded to people. Whilst there was a benefit in carrying out a restructuring of the organisation, unless the consultant and the participants identified and dealt with the relationship problems, these problems would remain and simply surface elsewhere in the new structure.

Reviewing How The Diagnostic Stage Is Going

At every stage in your relationship with a consultant you should review how the relationship is going — both formally and informally. There are three reasons for this.

Firstly, it is important that you and the consultant feel the work is going the way you want it to. You need to assess the extent to which the consultant is doing what you expected and doing so in a way that reflects the values you understood were agreed. Is the consultant behaving in ways that have integrity, feel empowering and create ownership? If you are concerned about what the consultant is doing or how, then you should raise it with them.

The consultants, too, might want to renegotiate the contract as it proceeds. If the consultants feel, for example, that in the light of what they have found to date they want to interview other people in the organisation that were not included in the original contract, then this should only be done through a review and an agreement. If you want the consultant to undertake further information collection such as more meetings with other agencies, then raise this suggestion and negotiate it with them.

A second and very different reason for reviewing your relationship with the consultant is that it will reveal information about how you, personally, or your organisation as a whole deal with problems. Consultants will pay a lot of attention to how you treat them. This is not only because they are concerned to ensure the consultancy is successful but because the way you handle the consultant gives them information about how you might deal with other people and problems in your organisation. This is important information that the consultant will use to diagnose action in order to help resolve the 'technical' problem. This can be done quite openly. The consultants may draw attention to how you deal with them to illustrate a problem they have identified about how you are handling the technical problem.

The consultant had been asked to help a social work staff team improve the quality of their practice in dealing with child abuse cases. The consultant found that when at the start of the contract he began analysing the existing practice his credibility as a consultant kept being questioned. After clarifying his knowledge and experience twice, the consultant asked the staff team to reflect on what their rejection of him revealed about their attitudes to accepting new ideas and new ways of working generally. This focus on the relationship between the consultant and the team enabled them to examine the cause of their defensive behaviour towards other agencies and practice developments. This led to a positive discussion about relationships with other staff teams and other organisations which in turn created a more open approach to improving the quality of their practice.

Thirdly, in reflecting on your relationship with the consultant, are there aspects of his or her behaviour that could be a model for you to use in the way you and others are relating to each other? Do they use techniques such as writing on flipcharts for recording views that you could use in your meetings? Do they have ways of intervening that assist group discussion that you could adopt such as asking for a round of opinion?

Techniques For Gathering Information

In order to make a diagnosis of the problem, its causes and how it is being dealt with, you and the consultant need to gather together a variety of facts, opinions, statistics, assumptions, clues, signs and signals. It is unlikely that one method of collecting such information will be sufficient or appropriate. The six methods that consultants frequently use are:

   i)   Interviews – individually or with groups
   ii) Group activities
  iii) Written questionnaires
  iv) Written diagnostic tools
   v) Document analysis
  vi) Observation

The tender for a strategic review in Appendix 2 combines a variety of these information collection methods.

Consultants will also use their own experience of working with you as a significant source of information about you and how you handle problems.

The choice of which combination of information gathering methods to use will depend on some key questions:

- What methods will give us the best information we need to achieve the analysis?
- How many people need to be involved or consulted?
- Should everyone be involved, or a sample?
- How much time do we have?
- How much will it cost?
- What methods fit our culture as an organisation?
- What effect will doing the data collection have on the organisation?

It is not the purpose of this section to describe which methods for collecting information are appropriate — this will vary enormously according to the consultancy task. But there are some useful points to bear in mind when considering the use of interviews, group activities, questionnaires, diagnostic tools, document analysis and observation.

• Interviews

Individual Interviews Consultants often use individual interviews or face-to-face meetings as their primary method for gathering information. It is seen as a valuable way of discovering people's attitudes, values and opinions and, more importantly, as a two-way process between you and them that will help to identify something new about the problem that can lead to action to resolve it.

If there was a simple solution to the problem, you would have probably identified it already (or rejected it as a solution for some reason that the consultant needs to discover). So the consultant will want to conduct the interview in a way that gives greater clarity about the issues and reveals deeper layers of the problem.

Information gathering interviews can be done in different ways:

- They can include closed questions that require you to give a yes/no or easily categorised response — eg. "How would you describe the climate of the organisation — Excellent, Satisfactory, Poor or Very Poor?"

- They can be a series of pre-set open questions that allow you to be more unconstrained in your response — eg. "How would you describe the working atmosphere in the team?
- Or they can be a deeper exploration of the problem being looked at, taking the form of a more open-ended but structured discussion focusing on those aspects with which the interviewee is most competent to comment on.

The closed and pre-set open questions are often used in telephone interviews where the lack of personal contact makes greater exploration more difficult.

Figure 25 summarises three layers that a consultant might seek to work through during a more exploratory diagnostic interview. He will begin with asking about the 'presenting problem', move on to your perceptions about how other people are contributing to the problem, and finally arrive at what you are doing that contributes to the problem. Each of these layers interact and the consultant will want to explore, for example, your working relationship with others in the organisation.

Resistance to Analysis   Working through these layers is not a mystical process that you should be suspicious of. It is a process to give the consultant the information they need to make a useful diagnosis; a process to give you insights into the problem for yourself; and a process that will give you an indication of what the consultant is thinking is the important problem to be worked on.

You can analyse your own behaviour when being interviewed to consider whether you are really working with the consultant to explore the problem fully or whether you are consciously or unconsciously resisting the process:

- Am I only talking about the behaviour of others and resisting talking about me, my behaviour and my contribution to the problem?
- Am I tending to go off on side issues and diverting attention away from the real issue?
- Am I being silent or giving very short answers and avoiding the questions?
- Am I going into too much detail and so clouding the issue?
- Do I keep saying I'm confused about why this interview is happening even though it's been explained to me twice?
- Am I moralising about other people and what they should be doing rather than thinking about the fact that I disagree with them and how my conflict with their views can be dealt with?

If you are not reflecting on how you are responding to the interview, the consultant will be. They will be trying to help you avoid responding in these ways by restating something you've said, disclosing a similar experience, asking open-ended questions and testing out how you might be feeling.

If they believe your response to the interview is resistance, they may name that resistance — describe what they see you doing — as a means of helping you to reflect on your behaviour and return to the problem.

Group Interviews and Discussion   The group interview and discussion reveals information in two ways — the content that people give and the process or behaviour in the group. As with individual interviews, the group discussion is a valuable way of exploring values, attitudes and opinions, and for getting into deeper layers about the problem and its causes.

If the group are a team in your organisation — or a group of managers who need to work together — then the behaviour in the group could well provide more important information about the problem than what they say. But if the group have been drawn together for a discussion to simply save time, the diagnosis may be of less importance.

Layer	Consultant's Question	Issue Being Explored
Top	What's the technical or business problem you are experiencing?	The presenting problem will most often be expressed in organisational or technical terms: "We aren't achieving our aims, my group isn't going well, the system isn't working".
Second	What are other individuals or groups in the organisation doing to either cause or maintain this problem at its current level of severity?	The person's perceptions about how others are contributing to the problem is the next level. "People are more interested in the processes than the product of this organisation, two members of the group do all the talking, the people don't understand the system".
Third	What is your role in the problem? What is there in your approach to ways of dealing with the situation that might be contributing to the problem or getting in the way of its resolution?	This is a statement of how a person sees his or her own way of contributing to the problem. The person may be contributing by certain conscious actions or by simply not giving the problem attention. It is vital as it brings responsibility closer to the person involved. Instead of expressing the situation in terms of forces outside the person which are creating problems, the focus is moved a little more internally.

Adapted from Peter Block (5)

Figure 25:   Layers of Analysis

The consultant can lead a group interview in the same way as a one-to-one interview using closed or open questions in a structured or unstructured way to explore different layers of the problem. The group dynamics may mean that this is a harder task as the consultant seeks to ensure that everyone has a chance to give their viewpoint and different people resist the exploration in different ways at different times. The consultant may name these resistances and ask the participants to reflect on how the group is working and what this might reveal about the way they handle problems.

A diagnostic group discussion should not be confused with a group planning an implementation process. The purpose is different and the process will be different too. However, it is often the case that once a group has begun to share information and views and analyse their responses, they may be in a position and mood to identify options and agree ways forward.

Consultants may want to use techniques that encourage group discussion and analysis. Examples of techniques that can be used for a group information sharing and analysis of a problem include:

- **Brainstorming**: People are encouraged to give ideas or viewpoints that are written down on flipchart paper without being challenged. This list is then discussed, key areas highlighted, issues that fall into similar categories marked, and so on.
- **Structured Brainstorming**: People discuss their views or thoughts in pairs and the points are written up one point per pair until all the issues are identified.

- **Rounds**: Each person is invited in turn to say what their view is about the issue, or the process that is happening in the group.
- **Talking Walls**: A series of open or closed questions are written up on flipcharts for people to walk round and complete. The information is then discussed by the group as a whole, or a subgroup takes the answers from a section of the wall and prepares a summary of the findings to feedback.
- **Index Cards**: There are many ways of using index cards in groups for exploring problems depending on the size of the group and the outcome desired.

  One method is

  (a) Each person write down on each of three cards three reasons why they think the problem exists. These are laid out on a table or floor so that everyone can see them.

  (b) Everyone pick up two cards that they think are the two most important causes of the problem. If their first two choices are picked up by someone else, they can pick up just one or none at all.

  (c) Lay out again the cards that have been chosen (the rest are discarded) and everyone turn over any card they disagree with or which they want clarified. All the cards left uppermost are statements of the cause of the problem that everyone agrees with — these should be written up on a sheet of flipchart paper.

  (d) The group should then work through each of the turned over cards with the person who wrote it saying why they think it is a cause of the problem and the person who turned it over responding to this point. The card is then either added to the list of agreed statements, amended and added, or listed as a point of disagreement.

• Group Activities And Exercises

Group physical activities that reveal information about a problem are commonly used in consultancy for diagnosing issues relating to team development but could be more widely applied.

One example is called 'sculpting' whereby the people in a group place themselves around a room in positions and stances that reflect a particular theme such as power that they want to explore. This kind of activity can have considerable impact and needs to be handled carefully by consultants with experience of working on questions of group work and team relationships. Three examples are given below:

> The consultant helped the team to diagnose their working relationships by assisting them to 'sculpt' themselves and review the outcome. This meant members of the team arranging themselves around the room in different stances and positions to reflect how they perceived power to be located in the team – the nearer the centre of the room, the more power. The consultant helped the team to discuss the 'sculpt' and air their perceptions about what it showed about formal and informal decision-making and communication within the team, and to identify ways of developing better working relationships.

> The consultant asked the team to arrange the furniture and themselves to reflect their relationship with the volunteers and committees in their organisation. The physical distance between the staff and the chairs, and the position of the organisation's Director, graphically illustrated why there were problems of lack of trust and confidence between staff and the rest of the organisation — an issue that might not otherwise have been so readily identified, but having done so could no longer be avoided.

A variation on this sculpting theme is to use drawing. The consultant asked each member of the team to draw a picture of the team with each person being a petal and the size and position of the petal representing their influence in the team.

Each person then presented their picture explaining who each person was in the picture and why they had drawn them that way. The difference in perception based on these drawings provided a useful starting point to resolve issues of the way people operated in the team and how others reacted.

The major benefit of sculpting and drawing is that they show simply and easily the complex problem which people find difficult to express verbally. The physical nature of the activity also makes it more memorable and is a shared experience to which people can readily refer back to in later discussions.

• Written Questionnaires

Simple written questionnaires asking for facts or opinions are a tool often used by consultants for gathering information. They can be used among a small group of staff to give the consultant some written comments that can be followed up in individual interviews or group discussions and activities (see Appendix 3) or to canvass the views of a wider range of people such as the users of a service (see Appendix 4). Their design, distribution and analysis all depend on the nature of the consultancy task being undertaken. The decisions about the questions asked, the style of the questions asked and who is asked to complete them are decisions that themselves reveal information about your organisation, the 'technical' problem you want to resolve and how you are dealing with it.

Appendix 4 is an example of a questionnaire used to gather young views in a review of a community project. It includes 'open' questions and closed (tick-the-box or circle the answer) questions. The questionnaire was piloted on a few young people before proper distribution. The decision to survey young people's views came late in the process of choosing who to collect information from and the staff recognised this was a significant indicator of the project's approach to young people's involvement in the decision-making.

One dilemma in the use of survey questionnaires is the undue weight that can be placed upon them. Once the information is analysed and presented in graphs it can gain a status that places it above the 'softer' data of observation and interviews, even though it may not be complete or in sufficient depth. To avoid this it is important to place the survey results alongside all the relevant information about a particular area of concern, to draw out only the key aspects of that information and to use judgement with integrity in analysing the data and drawing conclusions.

• Written Diagnostic Tools

Written diagnostic tools are also used by many consultants when seeking to understand the nature of the problems in the organisation. Although a pen-and-paper procedure, they differ from ordinary questionnaires which need you to analyse and interpret the information you collect. Written diagnostic tools contain a diagnosis within their structure. It asks you questions and then interprets your answers.

Some consultancy organisations have developed highly sophisticated questionnaires that are analysed in detail and used by them as 'concrete' evidence to present to you a description of your problems and what is causing them. A note of warning is needed here. Consultants differ markedly in their approach to such diagnostic tools. Some view them as telling 'the truth' and believe that variables such as different organisational settings, cultural differences among the participants or simply people's mood when completing them have been taken into account through extensive field testing of their content and use. Others are more sceptical and use such instruments only as an additional way of gathering insights into the overall picture being built up through interviews, observation and so on.

Whether seen as 'telling the truth' or as another way of gaining some insights within a variety of information gathering methods, it is important that such diagnostic tools are not used to place the consultant in some special position of being the person with mysterious knowledge or mystical analytical powers. That does not empower the participants and is likely to reinforce their dependency on the consultant. Two examples of such diagnostic tools are given below and on page 73.

> An example of a simple diagnostic tool used to help small voluntary projects gain an overall picture of themselves is given in Appendix 5. Staff and committee members each completed a brief questionnaire and used the results to plot a profile of their organisation on to individual sheets and then one large wall chart. The lower the score on the profile the more this area of the organisation might need some attention. And the differences in the profiles between people from the same organisation also raises useful areas for discussion.
>
> The questionnaire and the analysis was all done by the participants – not taken away to be compiled by the consultant and presented as fact. So participants who thought the profile did not match their perceptions of the organisation could go back to the questions and the process to see what it was that caused the result.

● Document Analysis

Depending upon the nature of the task, consultants may want to see your published documents such as annual reports, newsletters and so on; and internal documents such as minutes of meetings, internal reports, policy statements and so on.

They may have a specific aspect in mind when reading them such as the images portrayed (do pictures show examples of men and women in non-stereotyped roles; are they multicultural, etc.); the content (does the policy reflect best practice etc.), factual data (statistics, budget, staffing levels, participation rates etc.).

Or they may wish to gain a more general picture of what your organisation is about and how it has developed over a period of time, as evidenced by your published and unpublished material.

Analysing documents is also a way for consultants to develop an understanding of how your organisation communicates internally and externally and makes decisions — the types of documents you produce, what internal memos are used for, what is filed and how, what is recorded at meetings and why, who has access to written information, and so on.

> A consultant was used by an environmental voluntary agency to develop ways of increasing usage by minority groups. The publications of an environmental voluntary agency — posters, leaflets, booklets etc. — were looked at to assess the extent to which their presentation reflected participation by minority groups and the topics/issues addressed reflected the experiences and interests of Black and Asian people. This led to changes in both the images used and the aims and services of the organisation.

The publication *Improving Work Groups: A Practical Manual For Team Building* by D. Francis and D. Young (10) contains a team review questionnaire that teams can use on their own or with a consultant to identify blockages to their team's development. This diagnostic tool enables teams to identify areas of concern from twelve key aspects of effective teamwork:

1. **Appropriate Leadership.** The team manager has the skills and intention to develop a team approach and allocates time to team-building activities. Management in the team is seen as a shared function. Individuals other than the manager are given the opportunity to exercise leadership when their skills are appropriate to the needs of the team.

2. **Suitable Membership.** Team members are individually qualified and capable of contributing the "mix" of skills and characteristics that provide an appropriate balance.

3. **Commitment to the Team.** Team members feel a sense of individual commitment to the aims and purposes of the team. They are willing to devote personal energy to building the team and supporting other team members. When working outside the team boundaries, the members feel a sense of belonging to and representing the team.

4. **Constructive Climate.** The team has developed a climate in which people feel relaxed, able to be direct and open, and prepared to take risks.

5. **Concern to Achieve.** The team is clear about its objectives, which are felt to be worthwhile. It sets targets of performance that are felt to be stretching but achievable. Energy is mainly devoted to the achievement of results, and team performance is reviewed frequently to see where improvements can be made.

6. **Clear Corporate Role.** The team has contributed to corporate planning and has a distinct and productive role within the overall organisation.

7. **Effective Work Methods.** The team has developed lively, systematic and effective ways to solve problems together.

8. **Well-Organised Team Procedures.** Roles are clearly defined, communication patterns are well developed, and administrative procedures support a team approach.

9. **Critique Without Rancour.** Team and individual errors and weaknesses are examined, without personal attack, to enable the group to learn from its experience.

10. **Well-Developed Individuals.** Team members are deliberately developed and the team can cope with strong individual contributions.

11. **Creative Strength.** The team has the capacity to create new ideas through the interactions of its members. Some innovative risk taking is rewarded, and the team will support new ideas from individual members or from outside. Good ideas are followed through into action.

12. **Positive Intergroup Relations.** Relationships with other teams have been systematically developed to provide open personal contact and identify where joint working may give maximum pay-off. There is regular contact and review of joint or collective priorities with other teams. Individuals are encouraged to contact and work with members of other teams.

The authors state that their questionnaire does not tell objective truth but that the reported information is clearly subjective. They then provide exercises and activities that teams can use to help them analyse and resolve the areas needing most attention — again with or without a consultant.

● Observation

Depending on the nature of the task, consultants will very often find it useful to observe what your organisation does and how it is managed. Although 'expensive' in the time it takes, observation gives the consultant first-hand information that can be reviewed and discussed later as a shared experience.

Both you and the consultant need to be clear about why the consultant is there and what is being observed. Other people need to be told in advance that the consultant will be attending and why. You may need to introduce the consultant and explain her presence at the start of the session. You need to have agreement about whether the consultant will make notes or in other ways record what they are observing at the time or afterwards; and how these observations will be used.

The presence of consultants will affect what happens. What they observe may not be 'representative' of what happens every day. This is not necessarily a bad thing. You may find that a meeting that is normally a disaster goes very well in the presence of a consultant. This is the time to ask what was different. What did you do in front of the consultant that you don't normally do. More importantly, what did you *not* do that normally happens. In this way you can use the effect of the observer's presence to produce learning and, hopefully, change for the better — a good use of consultants.

Funnelling, Summarising and Analysing the Information

This is the tricky bit. There is a pile of interview notes, a stack of questionnaires that have been analysed, the write-ups from some group discussions, a box of internal documents that have been read, a file of relevant statistical data and the notes from observing a series of staff meetings. What happens now?

The task is to funnel, summarise and analyse the information in order to focus on the key items that are important to the organisation, can be changed by the organisation, and which people in the organisation want to change.

One approach is to take each of the key issues to be addressed and summarise the main points and facts about that issue that have been gathered via the different information collection methods. There is an element of 'living with the data' for a period until you (or the consultant) can see the patterns within it. Having summarised them, analyse them to develop suggestions for action or ways forward on dealing with them – a process that is often better done by two or more people together (see Figure 26).

You might expect consultants to be very rigorous in applying detailed and systematic approaches to analysing the information they have collected. But most avoid this approach.

> ❝ Despite the advanced statistical methods available, OD practitioners [Organisational Development consultants] in one survey reported giving the data only the simplest analysis. Specifically, in over 80 per cent of the projects the data was either 'eyeballed' or subjected only to simple statistics to analyse the data. ❞ Harvey and Brown (11)

The reason for this is to repeat that consultancy is not research. It is about making a judgement about what is important — not being comprehensive or overly detailed. This is summed up in the way one consultant described his approach:

> ❝ You always collect more data than you could ever use. A high anxiety point in any consulting project of any length is when you have finished asking your questions, have all the information you are going to get, and now have to make sense out of it.
>
> You may have devised a rational, logical process to sort out and categorize the data, but the selection of what is important is essentially a

judgement on your part. This is what they are paying you for. Trust your intuition, don't treat it as bias. If you are an internal consultant, you are often familiar with all the organisation, the people and how they operate. Use this information in condensing the data.

When I am struggling to decide what is important in a pile of notes, I will sometimes read through all the notes once, then put them away. On a blank sheet of paper I will then list what I think is important in the data — usually about four or five items. I let that be my guide on what to report and how to organise the report. I have faith that what I can remember is what is really important. Since a person can only absorb a limited amount of data, what stands out to me is what I want to stand out to the client. Let the information that stays in the background become part of an appendix, but don't clutter the feedback meeting with a complete list of everything you found out. " (5)

That approach may seem simplistic but it reflects the essence of what consultancy is about — not research, and not justification, but focusing on the key items that are important, can be changed and which people want to change.

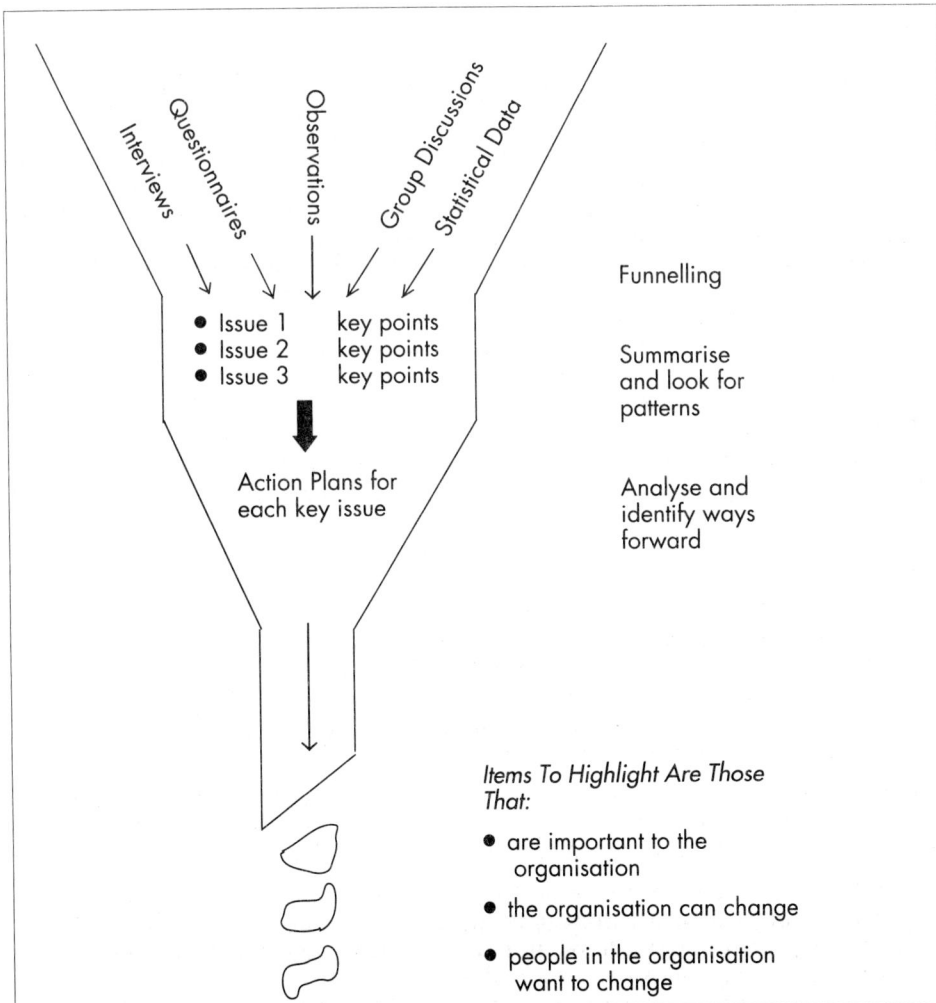

Figure 26.   Funelling, Summarising and Analysing The Information

Diagnostic Dilemmas

You should be aware of some of the pitfalls that can occur in the diagnostic phase of a consultancy contract — whether it is done by yourself facilitated by a consultant, jointly with a consultant or by the consultant alone. The main dilemmas to resolve in the diagnostic process are:

- The time and cost
- Appropriate methods
- Contamination
- Over-diagnosis
- Under-diagnosis
- Crisis diagnosis
- Threatening diagnosis
- Favourite diagnosis
- Culturally-based diagnosis

Adapted from Harvey and Brown (11)

● Time and Cost

Whilst interviews can be very effective they are expensive in both the amount of your time it takes and the costs of the consultant. They also create administrative and travel costs in setting them up and doing them.

You should not under-estimate the amount of written information you already have that is relevant to the problem and that you should make available to the consultant. Your time is not taken up whilst the consultant is reading. Similarly, consultant observation of your meetings or work does not take up more of your time but can give a lot of information to a consultant about what goes on in your organisation, how people behave and how problems are dealt with.

You and the consultant need to be sure that given the time and money available there is a combination of information collection methods that will generate the information required to make a reasonably accurate diagnosis.

● Appropriate Methods

Some methods of collecting information such as sculpting or using a written diagnostic tool may feel wholly inappropriate to your organisation's culture. You and the consultant have a choice — to avoid such methods because they seem to be inappropriate or to deliberately use such methods to begin to counter the prevailing culture. Using new ways of working is a common approach for creating change at the stage of implementation but carries the risk of increased resistance when used in the initial diagnostic stage of a consultancy. It also directly affects what is happening in your organisation and quickly generates change.

● Contamination

Purposefully using 'inappropriate' methods of information collection highlights the dilemmas that the very act of investigating, asking questions and observing will influence the behaviour of the participants — the Hawthorne effect, named after the researcher who first highlighted this dilemma. By asking basic questions about why people do what they do, the consultant is stimulating thinking and inevitably creating change. If consultancy is viewed as research, this is a dilemma. Researchers usually try their hardest to avoid having any impact on what they are researching — this is viewed as contamination. But consultancy is not research; it is about giving advice and support in order to take action to resolve problems. The question is not how to avoid the information collection methods having an influence but to ensure they have an influence that is congruent with resolving the problem being addressed.

> A youth organisation wanted to make its services more relevant to today's generation and change the traditional approach of its staff to working with young people. It was suggested that an independent opinion poll of young people's views about the agency be carried out to support this change. Instead, the staff and the existing young users of the organisation themselves jointly carried out the opinion poll — a process that both collected information of relevance to the problem and was contrary to their existing approach of giving young people instruction.

● Over-diagnosis

There are two kinds of over-diagnosis. Firstly, too much time can be spent collecting information and analysing it and not enough time taking action to resolve the problems. It is important to get the balance right when planning the consultancy process and to avoid the diagnosis itself becoming a ritual of continual analysis.

Secondly, several problems might be identified that need to be resolved. But if there are too many things to tackle and too many alternatives about how to approach them, you can lose sight of what are the most important ones and which need to be dealt with first. To avoid this, concentrate on funnelling the information so as to focus on the key areas, summarise them and be clear about what the implications might be for future action.

● Under-Diagnosis

Arriving at a diagnosis and making recommendations for change on the basis of insufficient information can also be a difficulty. It is essential that you provide consultants with the information they need if you expect them to do a reasonable analysis. You have a lot of control both in determining the information collection methods and in being open with the consultants when they have started work. It can be easy to play games with the consultant by not giving them information you know is vital or, for example challenging the statistical validity of the data they do collect because you don't like the results. It is important to remember that the purpose of diagnosis is action, not research. Unlike research, consultancy means drawing on both 'hard' and 'soft' data and mixing it with personal judgements to arrive at a diagnosis.

> In a review of one organisation the consultants used a variety of methods for finding out people's views about that organisation. One method was a questionnaire to gather the opinion of other organisations. Only a relatively low percentage of forms were returned. The consultants made a diagnosis of the organisation drawing on a range of data including interviews, group discussions and the questionnaire returns. But the analysis and recommendations were rejected by the organisation on the grounds that the sample size from the questionnaires made the results statistically invalid.
> The problem was two-fold. The consultants had not ensured that the organisation was jointly involved in the diagnosis and data collection process. And the organisation treated this part of the process as research rather than action-oriented diagnosis.

● Crisis Diagnosis

Consultants can fall into the trap of responding to the immediate crises they see. They are often eager to help you to solve problems and in conducting their interviews or group discussions could be diverted away from the underlying problems by the short-term and very visible issues they meet. As a result they could miss the longer term, underlying problems and concentrate on what may only be symptoms. In analysing the information collected you and the consultant need to feel able to 'get up into the helicopter' and look at the overall picture of what is happening. Action should be focused on the factors that are causing the symptoms rather than on responding to the immediate problems presented.

● The Threatening Diagnosis

The extent and depth of change required in some organisations to ensure their survival can be dramatic. But you and the consultant you use want to avoid a situation in which the consultancy operation is a success but your organisation dies. It is of little value if the changes, or the ways in which the consultants present their proposals for change, are so overwhelming and dramatic that the organisation suffers badly. You and the consultant need to avoid coming up with radical solutions in order to justify the time and money spent on the consultancy. There is a truth in the saying 'If it's not broken don't fix it'. And 'shock' tactics may have unexpected and unwanted side effects.

A different kind of threatening diagnosis is one that imposes an alien set of organisational 'cultures' on to your agency. You should not deliberately avoid 'threatening' change or change that requires a massive shift in your organisation's culture. But unless you have specifically asked for a particular approach to be taken, you should expect consultants to at least map out several options and their implications, one of which might require fundamental change.

> " The recommendation that is philosophically unacceptable is more serious — such as asking an arts group to start charging fees when its whole purpose is to provide free access; proposing a hierarchical management structure in a collective enterprise; or suggesting volunteers should be phased out in favour of fewer but full-time paid staff to make an organisation more efficient. It is not that such against-the-grain recommendations should not be made — indeed, the challenge can shake up a complacent organisation and cause it to re-affirm its values and enable a confident one coherently to dismiss them. But they should be set out as one of several options with the implications of each described "
>
> Rick Rogers (6)

● The Favourite Diagnosis

In your exploratory meetings and in agreeing a contract with a consultant you may have already discovered her particular bias or way of looking at the organisational world. A dilemma that you and the consultant will need to consider is whether the diagnosis being made only reflects that original bias (and hence may be missing an important aspect) or endeavour to analyse the problem from a variety of viewpoints and approaches.

It may be that the tendency for consultants to use their favourite diagnosis is an inevitability. If a consultant always sees problems as rooted in structure, she will inevitably find structural solutions to the problem you have. If she views organisational problems as fundamentally to do with how people relate and communicate with each other, then don't be surprised when she recommends solutions based on improving relationships and team-building. And if she is an expert on re-organising services into devolved and competing profit centres, then do not expect proposals for services based on sharing resources towards co-operatively agreed plans.

● The Culturally-Biased Diagnosis

You and the consultant can fail to recognise that the diagnosis is culturally biased because it fails to take account of Black, womens or disabled peoples' perspectives. The original planning and contracting process should have raised this issue. And the way the consultancy is carried out should ensure that any obvious pitfalls are avoided by collecting the views of individuals and groups inside and possibly outside the organisation who reflect these perspectives. The feedback and action planning phase also provides an important opportunity to check out and remedy any bias. You or the consultant may feel it is impossible to or even undesirable to eliminate some 'cultural' bias in which case this needs to be acknowledged with clearly stated reasons.

DIAGNOSIS AND INFORMATION GATHERING
KEY POINTS

1. Diagnosis is the process of understanding and describing the issue or problem you want to address.
2. The purpose of diagnosis is to create action about a problem. Diagnosis in a consultancy is *not* the same as research which has understanding rather than action as its purpose.
3. The basic steps in carrying out the diagnosis are:
   1. Identifying The Presenting Problem
   2. Choosing A Limited Number Of Areas To Be Examined
   3. Deciding Who Will Be Involved
   4. Choosing How The Information Will Be Collected
   5. Collecting The Information
   6. Funnelling, Summarising And Analysing The Information
4. The consultant and you will have different starting points. Whatever diagnosis you have done, the consultant will want to continue to explore deeper and deeper layers of the problem you want to tackle. That's their job.
5. The consultant's primary concern is to get a good diagnosis *and* ensure you own it.
6. You have three choices:
   - **Self-Diagnosis** in which the consultant facilitates you to undertake your own diagnosis.
   - **Joint Diagnosis** in which you and the consultant both contribute a diagnosis of the problem.
   - **Independent Diagnosis** in which the consultant does the diagnosis and gives you the results.
7. The consultant and you need to be diagnosing both the problem and how you are dealing with the problem.
8. You should review with the consultant how the diagnostic stage is going to ensure you both feel the work is going the way you want it to; to reflect on how your relationship with the consultant gives information about how you deal with problems in your organisation; to use aspects of the relationship as a model for you to use in your organisation.
9. The main techniques for gathering information are:
   i) Interviews – individually or with groups
   ii) Group Activities
   iii) Written Questionnaires
   iv) Written Diagnostic Tools
   v) Document Analysis
   vi) Observation
10. When you and/or the consultant is funnelling, summarising and analysing the information collected, it is important to focus on items that:
    1. Your organisation has control over changing
    2. Are clearly important to your organisation
    3. There is some commitment somewhere in your organisation to work on the item.
11. The main dilemmas to resolve in the diagnostic process are:
    - The time and costs
    - Appropriate methods
    - Contamination
    - Over-diagnosis
    - Under-diagnosis
    - Crisis diagnosis
    - Threatening diagnosis
    - Favourite diagnosis
    - Culturally-biased diagnosis

Feedback, Action-Planning and Implementation

What is Feedback?

● The Purpose of Feedback is Action

Unless you have contracted with consultants for them to act solely as facilitators, you will want to receive feedback from them about the problem being addressed.

The purpose of feedback is for you to receive information and to make a commitment to act. You should expect the consultant to present a clear picture of the current situation and their recommendations. The consultant will be encouraging you to focus on doing something about the problem.

● Types Of Feedback

Feedback may be a written report, a written summary or verbal feedback. It may happen once, on two or three occasions as part of a regular cycle of doing-reviewing-implementing (see Figure 27), or live as the situation demands. It may be a formal meeting or it could be an informal discussion. Your choice of feedback will depend largely on the nature of the consultancy task and the preferences of the consultant. A strategic review could require an essay-style written report or a lecture-style series of written sheets in bullet-point format presented on OHPs and collated together as a report. It could be done on flipchart paper and handouts to create a more collaborative approach and a 'working' atmosphere. Feedback during a team development process may be live 'on the days' as the consultant works with the team and makes observations on what is happening and suggestions about ways forward.

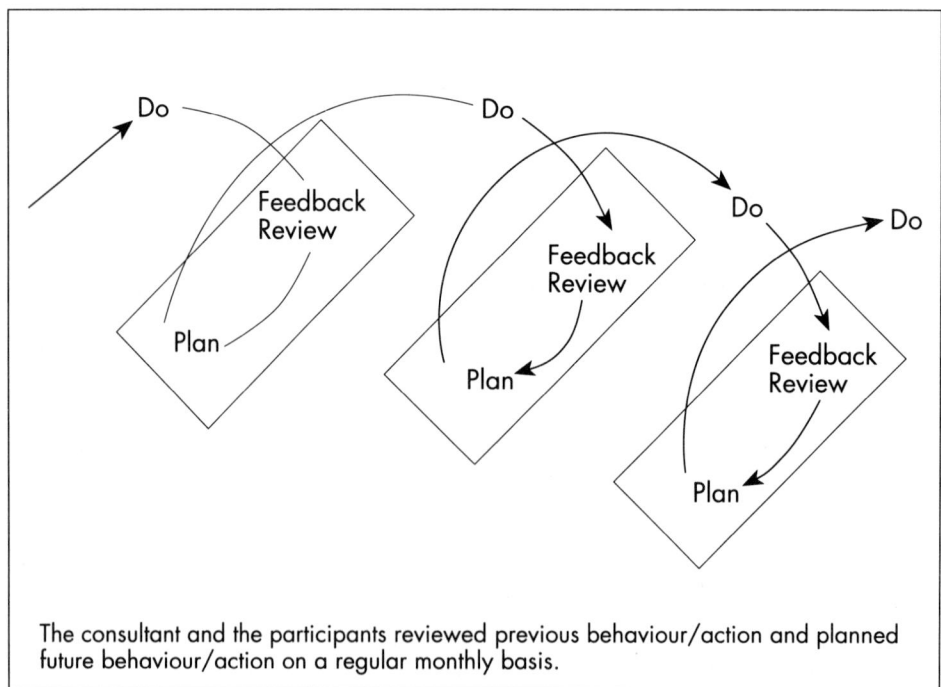

The consultant and the participants reviewed previous behaviour/action and planned future behaviour/action on a regular monthly basis.

Figure 27: The Do-Review-Plan Cycle

In one organisation the consultant met with different tiers of staff from administrative assistants to the Director in a series of one-day meetings. A 'cascade' was designed whereby the issues and problems for each tier were either resolved by that tier, or if they required a decision at a higher level were passed on to the next meeting via the consultant. The approach initially by the consultant was to hand out the written notes from one tier to the next tier for discussion. But this created enormous resistance and defensiveness. So a different approach was used where the consultant gave a flipchart presentation of the key points to the next tier. This was much more successful in enabling the 'receivers' not to react against the ideas but to explore the issues and respond positively. The material was the same but the way it was presented was different and created a different climate as a result.

● The Audience and Access to the Feedback

Feedback from a consultant is the opportunity for you to decide to take action, so who should be the audience?

You, and the consultant, need to decide who has access to any feedback from a consultant be it verbal or in a report. The decision about who has access is largely in your hands and it may be something you agreed with the consultant right at the start of the contract.

When making this decision the main groups of people to consider are:

1. **Those who have the power to make decisions about the action recommended** – unless these people directly receive the feedback from the consultant, commitment to do something is less likely.
2. **Those who are directly affected by the feedback and recommendations** You may not *have* to involve the staff, volunteers or committee members in the feedback given by the consultant but a decision not to do so gives big signals to them about your approach to handling the problem. Trade union involvement may be important and you have the option of the consultant giving presentations to the various relevant groups and concluding in a final presentation that includes their reactions.
3. **Those who have taken part in the consultancy** This may be a much wider group and you may feel it is impractical or may feel vulnerable as an organisation if copies of the full report were sent to all the external individuals and agencies who were involved in the information collection. However, circulating a summary of the key points will demonstrate your commitment to the process, your willingness to be open and your self-confidence about moving forward.

The tender for a strategic review in Appendix 1 describes how written feedback will be given at different stages in the review to different groups and specifies the size and level of detail that this feedback will contain, namely:

● Presentation of a 20 page interim report to a Review Group involving senior staff, committee members, local staff and users.
● Presentation of the amended interim report to groups of staff, volunteers and committee members around the country.
● Presentation of a 60 page draft final report to the Review Group.
● Presentation of the final report to the Senior Management Team.

The Content of Feedback

• The Problem and how you are dealing with it

The consultant will want to give you feedback on all aspects of the problem — both the technical aspects (eg. a suggestion for a new fundraising strategy) and how you are dealing with it (eg. the sexist behaviour of the male honorary treasurer who continually puts down the fundraising officer because she's a woman). If a written report is expected, you might request that the problems relating to how individuals are behaving are given verbally because of the damage that could be caused by putting it down on paper and it being widely circulated.

But this approach must not be used as a means of avoiding dealing with the issue. Indeed, it may be the case that, in the example given, unless the attitude of the treasurer changes and his working relationship with the fundraising officer improves, then any fundraising strategy will never get off the ground.

• Accuracy

Feedback, particularly a written report that contains factual inaccuracies, will create difficulties for you and the consultant. The debate you want to encourage within your organisation as a result of the consultancy needs to focus on the action proposed to resolve the problem — the recommendations that are being made. However, people will have less confidence and less motivation to consider options for change if the report they read is factually wrong in some way — even if the errors have no direct bearing on the recommendations. Such errors allow people to direct attention away from the core issues and the need for change. Make sure that before the report is presented you have a chance to put right any factual inaccuracies (and do not use this as a final chance to alter the consultant's recommendations to fit your prejudices!)

• The Level Of Detail

The level of detail you expect from a report should be understood at the start. Do you want highly-detailed, nitty-gritty descriptions, analysis and recommendations or an overview of the key issues and broad brush suggestions for change? The more information included in a report (as distinct from analysis and recommendations for action), the more chance there is that discussion will centre on the validity and accuracy of that information rather than on the issues identified as needing to be resolved. You and the consultant have a difficult judgement to make. Is there sufficient information upon which to justify the judgements and recommendations but not an overload that diverts attention?

> After a 9 month review of administrative and financial systems, the consultant produced a 160 page report with 130 recommendations. By the time the report was presented, some of it was out-of-date, some of it had already been implemented, some applied to people who had changed jobs, and some of it still needed further discussion so could not be implemented.

Expectations and Surprises

It is crucial that your expectations about the feedback you want are clear and agreed with the consultant. This should have been discussed during your negotiation of the consultancy contract. If the consultant gives feedback in a form or way you were not anticipating because of lack of clarity about what was expected, you could at best be disappointed and at worst have a serious problem to deal with.

The consultant interviewed each member of a staff team about the problems they were experiencing. He produced a written summary that was circulated in advance of a team meeting to plan action for change and improvement. The day before the meeting a member of staff rang to stop the consultant coming because of the anger and conflict generated by the report. The staff had expected a summary or agenda of the issues they needed to tackle and not a description of those issues and their possible causes. They felt their trust had been betrayed and did not want to carry on working with the consultant. The consultant felt the report was what the team had wanted, was angry at the rejection and concerned about the distress caused. A lack of clarity about the feedback that was expected led to a serious breakdown in the consultancy.

Surprises Consultants know they have failed in their task if they wait until the feedback meeting to worry about whether you will accept their diagnosis and recommendations. By that time in the process they should have a good idea of whether you share their analysis. The meeting, and in particular a report, should be a confirmation of something you both know needs to be resolved and is realistic, practicable and clearly understood by all concerned. Failing that, the consultant should know you will disagree with their views and be ready for a meeting in which you will 'agree to differ'.

Whilst what the consultant says may well be very challenging, you should not expect her to spring a big surprise on you at a feedback meeting. The way that the consultant conducts the interviews, group discussions and so on should indicate the direction of her thinking. As well as gathering views and exploring the issues, he will have been testing out reactions to different options and alternatives as to the problem, its causes and ways of resolving it.

> " If you have kept in close touch with the consultants then there should be few or no surprises. The report is merely consolidating what has already been flagged up by or even discussed in detail with the consultants. "
>
> Rick Rogers (6)

Feedback Meetings

If the consultancy contract is structured to include a separate session for receiving feedback (as distinct from live feedback during a team building session), then you should be clear about the style and structure you want for that meeting and be aware of how you and the consultant might behave.

• Style

Different consultants will have different approaches to giving feedback. Some will want to give a formal cut-and-dried presentation that you can accept or reject. Others will want to be more informal and see their presentation as something to be chewed over and amended. You should make clear the extent to which you want the feedback meeting as a collaborative discussion in which you can make suggestions and proposals of your own, prompted by what the consultant has to say; or whether you expect it to be a them-and-us approach where the consultant makes a presentation and you decide what to do.

• Structure

Whilst the nature of the feedback you receive will vary according to the consultancy task, the basic format and style of the feedback meeting can be planned in advance to make it as productive as possible. The consultant's objective is for you to agree with and take ownership of the recommendations. The key is to ensure that the feedback the consultant gives focuses on a few main points and avoids going into too much detail. A general format you might ask consultants to use is given in Figure 28.

ITEM	% Time
1. Re-state a summary of the original contract	
2. Describe the agenda for the meeting	} 5%
3. Present the diagnosis	
4. Present the recommendations	} 15%
5. Discussion of diagnosis	
6. Discussion of recommendations	} 30%
7. Review of the meeting so far	10%
8. Decisions and Action Planning	30%
9. Closure	10%

Adapted from Peter Block (5)

Figure 28:   Structure of a Feedback Meeting

Figure 28 suggests that the bulk of the time is spent by you discussing the diagnosis and recommendations, and then making decisions about what to do. Only a relatively small amount of time is allocated to presentation by the consultant.

Having a review of how the meeting is going half-way through it is important because if it is not going in the way you want, you should say so whilst there is time to do something about it.

The end of the feedback meeting is a chance to check that you have sufficient commitment to go ahead and to consider any future involvement you want by the consultant in the process.

● Behaviour

The Consultant's Behaviour   Consultants will be nervous at a feedback session because they are worried you will reject their findings and might criticise them personally. If they are anxious, they may assume you are anxious. This nervousness might surface as undue defensiveness about their diagnosis and recommendations. However, you should expect them not to be aggressive or submissive but to be assertive. Figure 29 illustrates how these differences might appear — non-verbally.

This assertive style means consultants telling you their views without putting you down or making themselves seem superior. It means they should not collude with you by avoiding difficult areas. It means they should present you with issues they know you will find hard to accept. And it means they should confirm where they believe things are going well.

Your Behaviour   Consultants expect you or others in the organisation to be resistant to their findings. If the problem was easy you wouldn't have brought in consultants to help you deal with it.

You have every right to disagree with the consultant's diagnosis and recommendations but that is not the same as behaving in ways that resist change or avoid taking action about the real problem. Some things you can *avoid* doing are playing games in feedback meetings. Here are some of the favourites you might find yourselves or others doing:

Submissive	Aggressive	Assertive
• Tone may be sing-song or whining	• Tone is sarcastic, sometimes cold	• Tone is middle range, rich and warm
• Over-soft of over-warm	• Strident, often shouting, rises at end	• Not over-loud or quiet
• Hesitant and filled with pauses	• Often abrupt, clipped	• Fluent, few awkward hesitancies
• Unreal smiles when expressing anger, or being criticised	• Eyebrows raised in amazement/disbelief	• Smiles when pleased
• Evasive	• Tries to stare down and dominate	• Frowns when angry
• Looking down		• Firm but not 'stare down'
• Hand-wringing	• Finger pointing	• Open hand movements (inviting to speak)

Source Unknown

Figure 29: Submissive, Assertive and Aggressive Behaviour

- **'Beat The Consultant'**
  You continually challenge, question or criticise the consultant with the purpose of blocking progress. There will be times, of course, when the competence or style of the consultant may need to be challenged, but this is only of value when the intent is to assist the process. It rarely is.
- **'Yes, but . . .'**
  You agree with what the consultant has recommended but continually find reasons why it wouldn't work. Victory is achieved when the consultant agrees the problem is insoluble.
- **'We've Tried That Before'**
  You dismiss suggestions or proposals for change by citing similar attempts from the past which failed. Particularly useful if you have deliberately kept this experience from the consultant during the diagnostic stage.
- **Immediate and Complete Acceptance**
  You instantly agree with everything but your commitment is only skin-deep. As soon as the consultant leaves the room you'll find reasons why it was not such a good idea after all.
- **'When did you last visit a family centre?'**
  You find reasons why the suggestions are unpractical and unworkable and ask whether the consultant's actually even worked in a family centre (or youth club or whatever the problem is related to).
- **'Give Me More Detail'**
  You keep asking for more and more detail about the information that's presented to avoid discussing the key issues and the recommendations.
- **'Not enough detail'**
  You condemn the findings as giving insufficient grounds on which to base a judgement but helpfully propose a delay whilst more data is collected. A tempting trap for some consultants who might need the work.
- **'Is that based on Likert's Lynch Pin Theory of Management?'**
  You move the discussion from action to solve the problem into an intellectual debate about theory. You might even be able to put down the consultant who has never heard of Likert but knows your current structure is falling apart.

The Consultant's Response The consultant's feedback, your response and the consultant's response to you is a key point in the whole process. It is the point at which the transfer of responsibility for action or work occurs from the consultant to you.

Consultants will respond to questions about their diagnoses and recommendations in good faith. Twice. If the same question appears a third time they will suspect it is resistance. So you can expect consultants to give two straightforward replies to your questions about issues such as level of detail, practicality, validity of the data and so on. But thereafter they are likely to interpret your questions as a way of avoiding the issue or problem, or as hidden disagreement with what they have said.

At this point they may name the resistance as it happens. They will describe what you are doing and say that it is a form of resistance rather than dealing with the issue. You should welcome this. It is not done to expose people or score points but is the consultant's way of assisting you to realise what is happening and to put the focus back on to the problem. If you disagree with the analysis or the recommendations, then say so clearly rather than play games to disguise your views.

When giving feedback to groups, the consultant will also try to respond to the concerns and anxieties of every individual. But they will be making a judgement about how much time and effort to invest in the one person or group who is continually resisting as compared to the many others who are taking ownership and want to move on.

Taking Action

The action you take as a result of a consultancy will depend on the task. You may take action on your own, having said goodbye to the consultant after receiving their feedback and planning what to do. Or you may have negotiated a specific role for the consultant in the action you are now ready to take. This can include ongoing consultancy support and progress reviews.

● Ongoing Consultancy Support

If you continue to use a consultant in the implementation phase, the one key task of a consultant is to offer you support. You have decided what to do and a consultant can support you in doing it. The way they can support you can vary from offering skills and knowledge about the issue, to offering skills and knowledge about the process of implementing change.

But there should be a shift (if it has not been happening from the start) from the consultant offering you knowledge about the issue to using their skills to support you in developing your own knowledge and implementing change.

The extent to which the consultant works to the principles of empowerment and reduces participants' dependency upon them is particularly evident in the implementation phase. If at your support and review meetings you are relying on your consultant to come up with the answers about what to do next, then the consultancy has failed. It has failed to help you develop the skills, knowledge and confidence to move forward on your own.

The consultant helped a small voluntary organisation to draw up a development plan that included a fundraising strategy. He was asked to attend the monthly committee meetings for the following year to give advice and support on its implementation. At every meeting whenever the question of fundraising came up, the consultant was asked to give specific suggestions such as how to phrase particular requests for grants, what Trusts to approach and so on. By the end of the year the committee were still entirely reliant upon the consultant for what to do about raising money. No-one on the

---

committee had been groomed or recruited to take on this role as a full member of the committee and others had not bothered to learn the do's and don'ts of good fundraising. When the consultant's contract was finished, the organisation was no further forward than the year before in being empowered to raise its own funding.

● Progress Reviews

One common use of consultants during the action phase is to facilitate a review of progress. They will have a genuine interest in how you have got on and because of their previous involvement may be in a good position to help you in a review.

You can arrange to meet with the consultant after a number of weeks or months to review progress and ask them to help you answer key questions such as:

- Did we do what we set out to do?
  If not, why not?
- Did we do things other than we agreed and planned?
  If so, why?
- Did our actions achieve the outcomes we intended?
- What other outcomes resulted from the changes we implemented?
- How well did we manage the process of change?
- What do others think about what happened — other staff, volunteers, users, committee members?

You can ask these questions at any time — not wait for a consultant. The valuable thing about inviting the original consultant back to facilitate a review of progress is that the consultant's starting point is where he last saw you. You will have moved on. Things will have changed. What you are doing in six months' time will seem natural to you and as though it was never different. But the consultant will remind you of where you were and what you planned to do then and assist you to track the path you have taken to where you are now.

Figure 30 gives five examples of the ways that consultants can support your actions:

● Implementation Dilemmas

Involving a consultant in the implementation stage creates its own set of potential dilemmas of which you should be aware:

The Consultant Becomes a Manager Involvement in implementation is the point at which you are most likely to find yourself asking a consultant to make that all-important shift from consultant to manager. Don't do it. They will no longer be your consultant if they start to take responsibility for implementation. If you do it then openly acknowledge that the person has changed roles and they are now a sub-contractor, a staff person or a manager and will be responsible for delivering this part of the project.

Letting Go of the Consultant Consultancy is giving advice or assistance to improve a situation. One of the consultant's goals should be to work themselves out of a job — to get you to a position where the situation is improved and you no longer need them. But you and the consultant may resist ending the relationship you have developed. You get security from the support she provides and the consultant enjoys the feeling of being needed and being paid. Even with people who call themselves consultants but who are simply providing a specialist sub-contracted service (rather than consultancy) such as parliamentary lobbyists, it is worth developing time limited contracts. At the end of the period of the contract the contract can then be reviewed and a decision taken to end, amend or continue the contract for a further period.

- Group Process Facilitator

  A consultant used their process skills to assist an organisation arrive at a new 5 year plan. They then met with an implementation group on a regular basis for the first 12 months to assist the participants develop their skills and confidence in implementing and amending the strategy, and to review progress.

- Skills Trainer

  A consultant used their conflict resolution skills to help staff decide what to do about improving the working climate in their organisation. The consultant was then asked to provide the training identified as being needed among staff and committee members in communication and negotiation skills.

- Non-Managerial Supervisor

  A consultant with specialist knowledge of management structures was used to draw up plans for a new structure with the organisation. The consultant then met with the Director on a regular basis to continue to develop their knowledge and skills in implementing the new structure and to review how it was working in practice.

- Team Development Consultant

  A consultant met with a team for several sessions at regular intervals. At each session participants had the opportunity to share their views and insights, reflect on them, use activities to develop and extend their skills and learning and prepare for a further period of practical action that could be reviewed at the next session. In this approach a cycle of do-review-plan was used in which the participants and the consultant moved from diagnosis to implementation and back to diagnosis over several sessions.

- Progress Reviewer

  The consultant facilitated a one-day review meeting for an organisation with whom she had worked before. The consultant began by reminding the participants of the agreements and action plans they made six months before. She then drew a line on a large piece of paper representing the six months that had passed and asked people to annotate that line with statements of their feelings about events that had happened over that period. This subjective picture of events was then referred to in a systematic analysis of what had actually happened.

Figure 30:   Ways that Consultants can Support your Actions

Deskilling the Staff   The presence of a consultant who brings specialist help or knowledge can imply that you and others in the organisation do not have the resources or competence to solve the problem. The role that you ask the consultant to play is crucial to ensuring that you make use of their expertise without making you feel de-skilled in the process.

Whilst consultants only have advisory status, their informal power will have an effect on the complex pattern of human relationships that already exist in your organisation. At every point, and particularly during the implementation stage, you should ensure the consultant recognises the impact of their presence and seeks to use it to empower you and others in the organisation. You cannot pretend they don't exist or don't have an impact but you can expect the consultant to work in ways that reinforce and support participants in carrying through their plans and not take them over.

Dealing With The Unexpected   Consultants are people who, like you, will get anxious when confronted with deep-rooted or fundamental problems in organisations. They too may lie awake at night if issues and problems emerge that they are not equipped to handle or if they find themselves in very bitter situations. When a consultant is confronted with a new or unexpected issue, they will make judgements about whether to:

- go with that issue of concern and give whatever help they can.
- stop the work on that issue and stay within the boundaries established by the contract.
- re-negotiate the contract to take in the new issue.
- create a balance between working on the new issue and keeping to the contract.
- disclose to the group their own fear/being out of their depth, and trust the group to deal with it.

When choosing what to do consultants will make a judgement about whether the unexpected issue is a diversion, or is so overwhelming it cannot be ignored, or whether the group will gain strength from their disclosure of anxiety. You can help the consultant to help you by recognising the dilemma, avoiding using the consultant as a scapegoat for the problem that has emerged, and stating how you are feeling and what you are experiencing.

FEEDBACK, ACTION PLANNING AND IMPLEMENTATION
KEY POINTS

1. Unless you have contracted to do otherwise, you will expect to get feedback from consultants about the problem they have been seeking to address with you.
2. The purpose of feedback from a consultant is for you to receive information and make a commitment to act. You should expect to receive a clear picture of the current situation and their recommendations.
3. Your choice of feedback will depend largely on the consultancy task — it may be a written report, a written summary or a verbal report. It may happen once, regularly as part of a cycle or 'live' as the situation demands.
4. You should be clear about who the audience is for the feedback and what is confidential. You should consider feedback being given to:

   - those who have the power to make decisions about the recommendations;
   - those who are directly affected by the feedback and recommendations;
   - those who have taken part in the consultancy.

5. Feedback should include information and recommendations about the problem *and* how you are dealing with it.
6. You should ensure feedback is factually accurate and that the level of detail you expect is clear from the start. You should not be given surprises or shock feedback by consultants.
7. You should be clear about the style and structure of feedback meetings. The consultant should behave assertively — not aggressively or submissively and you should avoid 'game playing' as a means of resisting the feedback.
8. When taking action you can either say goodbye to the consultant or continue to use them for support and reviewing progress. Ways that consultants can support you include

   - being a group process facilitator
   - providing skills training
   - non-managerial supervision
   - team development consultancy
   - progress reviewer

9. Involving a consultant in the implementation stages creates its own set of dilemmas of which you should be aware

   - the consultant becomes a manager
   - letting go of the consultant
   - deskilling the staff
   - dealing with the unexpected

Chapter seven

Evaluating Consultancy

Definition And Purpose Of Evaluation
- ■ Definition
- ■ Formative Evaluation
- ■ Summative Evaluation

What To Evaluate
- ■ Overview
- ■ The Product
- ■ The Process
- ■ The Outcome

Evaluation Method
- ■ Progress Reviews
- ■ Participant Feedback
- ■ User Feedback

What Are Your Options If It Goes Wrong?
- ■ Learn from the Experience
- ■ Withhold payment
- ■ Sue the consultant

Definition and Purpose of Evaluation

• Definition

Evaluation is the process by which a judgement is made about the value of a consultancy. It should be an integral part of agreeing the consultancy contract rather than thought about at the end as an added extra.

The kind of evaluation process you use will depend on why you want to do it. Two basic reasons for evaluating a consultancy are:

- To help change and develop the consultancy as it goes along — *formative* evaluation.
- To assess at the end whether the outcomes and process of the consultancy achieved what was intended — *summative* evaluation.

• Formative Evaluation

Evaluation that helps to modify the consultancy as it goes along involves both you and the consultant. At each consultancy stage — contracting, diagnosis, feeding back, planning and acting — you and the consultant together can be asking:

- how is this process going?
- is the outcome what we want and does the way we are working together feel right?
- what, if anything, do we want to change about what is happening, how it is being done, and the outcomes it is creating?

• Summative Evaluation

There is, potentially, a much wider audience for evaluation at the end of a consultancy. A summative evaluation is an assessment of whether the intended outcomes were achieved and whether these outcomes have been of value to you. The answers to these questions will be of interest to different people for different reasons:

- Committee members and funding bodies might want to know whether the consultancy was money well spent and to know whether the original problems have been sorted out.
- Managers and staff might want the evaluation to confirm their experience of the consultancy and to know what everyone else thought about it.
- Users might want to know how the outcome will affect them.
- The consultant might want to have their experience of the consultancy confirmed and both you and they will want to learn from that experience in order to do the next one better. An example of a feedback form for you to give to consultants at the end of a consultancy is given in Appendix 6.

Whilst most people will want a summative evaluation to take place (just because they think it should), it is formative evaluation that is of most value in ensuring that the consultancy achieves what you want it to. It is of less value to discover at the end that a particular approach didn't work. Realising this when it happened would have given time to change things to make it a success. Summative evaluation is optional but formative evaluation should be an integral part of every consultancy.

What To Evaluate

• Overview

In all consultancies there are three aspects you can evaluate:

The Product Most commonly at the end of a consultancy this is a report with recommendations, but it could also, for example, be the write-up of a team building event. In formative evaluation you would receive interim reports or first drafts on which you could give feedback and comment.

The Process The tasks that are undertaken as part of the consultancy — collecting information, diagnosing, action planning and implementation — and the way those tasks were carried out. These can be evaluated whilst they are happening in order to change them or at the end to decide whether to do it again that way in future.

The Outcome Evaluating what happens as a result of the consultancy falls into two categories:

- Evaluating changes to what you do after the consultancy.
- Evaluating the results of those changes.

These three aspects are inter-related as illustrated below:

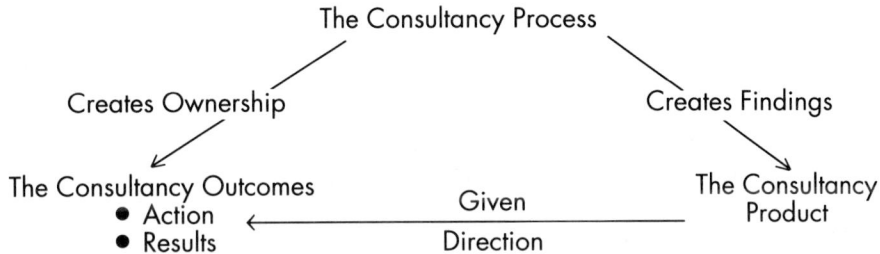

```
                    The Consultancy Process
              /                                \
    Creates Ownership                      Creates Findings

The Consultancy Outcomes                        The Consultancy
      • Action        <——————  Given  ——————       Product
      • Results              Direction
```

Figure 31 gives an example of these three areas being given a summative evaluation: the kinds of questions you could ask and what use you can make of the results. These three aspects of evaluation are now considered in more detail.

● The Product

A report with recommendations can readily be evaluated. The consultancy contract may have specified the length and style of report you want to receive:

> ❝ The review report will seek to reflect the strategic nature of the task. In practice this means that a relatively large amount of information is collected and then narrowed or distilled into the key findings, issues and options. It is important that the appropriate level of detail is included at the interim and final report stages. We envisage that the interim report will be no more than 20 pages in length and the final report no more than 60 pages in length ❞.
>
> Appendix 1

Figure 32 gives a list of possible criteria for evaluating consultancy reports and feedback:

If these evaluation criteria are applied to draft reports that can be amended, then these become formative evaluation questions that can change the final product.

● The Process

The processes you expect the consultant to use will also have been described in greater or lesser detail in the consultancy contract. They could include descriptions of:

	THE PRODUCT	THE PROCESS	THE OUTCOME	
			ACTION	RESULTS
EXAMPLE	A report describing the current practice in a project working with young people in trouble and making recommendations for change, and training for staff.	The consultant observed the practice, interviewed young people, facilitated a two-day practice review seminar, and wrote up the findings with reference to published examples of practice in other agencies.	The staff team received training in the new ways of working and put into action the approach that was agreed at the feedback and action planning meeting.	The numbers of young people in trouble who re-offend is reduced and fewer receive a custodial sentence.
EXAMPLE EVALUATION QUESTIONS	• Is the report clear and factually accurate? • Does it contain recommendations? • Is it based on the correct assumptions about our organisation?	• Do we own the new approach to practice that has emerged? • Do we have the confidence and commitment to put the changes into practice?	• Has the training given the staff the skills and knowledge they need? • Has the new practice been implemented?	• Has the recidivism rate gone down? • Has the seriousness of further offence been reduced? • Have fewer young people gone into prison?
HOW TO USE THE ANSWERS	• To confirm that the original contract was kept to.	• To decide whether to use a similar approach in future consultancies? • To decide whether to use the same consultants again?	• To review progress and plan further action to ensure change is implemented and maintained.	• To review practice • To ensure the changes to the practice achieve the outcomes we want and provide information for planning future practice.

Figure 31: Summative Evaluation of a Consultancy

- Is the length and style what was expected?
- Have different options been looked into?
- Is it factually correct?
- Are the assumptions made about the content, the organisation situation and the culture correct?
- Have the implications of different options been assessed?
- Is all the relevant information included?
- Does the information appear valid?
- Are clear recommendations given if required in the content?

Adapted from Rick Rogers (6)

Figure 32: Criteria for Assessing the Quality of a Report

- The information and diagnosis process
- The feedback and action planning process
- The implementation processes

The contract could also describe how these processes should affect you:

❝ The less visible but no less important outcome of the review is that there is ownership and commitment to the 5 year strategic plan that is produced at its conclusion ❞.

Appendix 2

You will want to evaluate whether these processes were undertaken and whether the way they were done achieved what you wanted. Whilst you should be concerned with issues about validity of the data and quality of the analysis, the questions that really matter are whether the consultancy process has enabled you to own the problem and be in a position to take action. The key questions about the consultancy process are:

- Are the key aspects of the problem being covered?
- Is the process going in the right direction?
- Am I feeling more or less dependent on the consultant?
- Am I feeling I have the skills and confidence to go forward on this course of action?
- Do I really 'own' what is going on or does it feel like the consultant is telling me what to do?
- Does the process feel 'off-the-shelf' or am I getting something that is tailor-made to my needs?
- Does the consultant share my social and political values, for example by demonstrating a commitment to social equality?
- Is the consultant behaving with integrity and being authentic?
- Am I being helped to think about the problem and how to deal with it or is the consultant simply giving me her solutions?

These questions too can and should be asked as the consultancy is in progress. Your replies can help the consultant to modify what he is doing and how he is doing it — even to renegotiate the contract if necessary. Such formative evaluation should be an integral part of the consultancy process.

- ## The Outcome

There are two types of outcome you can evaluate:

- Monitoring the implementation of your action plans
- Judging the results of those action plans

Monitoring Action Plans Changes to what you do is evaluated by monitoring whether or not things happen. It can be as simple as ticking off action plans that were made during the consultancy. If you have continued to use consultants for support during the implementation stage, then they may assist you to review what has happened and ask questions such as did we do what we said we would, and if not, why not? (see Chapter 6, Reviewing Progress').

Evaluating Results Evaluating the consultancy on the basis of the results of your action plans is arguably the most important but the hardest kind of evaluation to do. The problems are threefold:

Firstly, you may not know at the start what 'outcome' results you want to achieve. There may be a deep-rooted conflict about the outcomes you want which the consultancy is seeking to clarify.

The 'results' outcomes of the strategic review outlined in Appendix 1 were deliberately broad because one purpose of the review was to clarify what its aims and users were. Nonetheless, included at the start was a description of some longer-term results that the review might achieve:

> " In the longer term the review should result in:
> - more involvement of people from all sections of the community, especially those in different age ranges.
> - existing examples of excellent practice becoming the national standard.
> - new attitudes and commitment among staff and volunteers to undertake a wider range of areas of community action. "

Secondly, the results you want to achieve at the start may change as the consultancy proceeds — different issues and new outcomes might emerge that you want to work towards. This could make evaluation of whether you achieve the original outcomes a redundant exercise. And thirdly, there is a long chain of cause-and-effect between the consultancy intervention in your organisation and the impact on the ground. A good consultancy process may not result in clear, measurable outcomes. This makes use of the results as a means of evaluating the consultancy very difficult.

This is not to argue for avoiding setting such objectives or evaluating them, but to recognise that it won't be easy. You should try at the start to describe the longer term set of results that you hope the consultancy will achieve. And you should plan a means of assessing whether these have been achieved or whether new outcomes are now being aimed for.

Evaluation Methods

• Progress Reviews

Consultancy based around the principles of empowerment and independence will include regular times when review questions are asked. Such regular reviews may be formally timetabled into the process or take part more informally during group discussion, interviews and so on. It will be going on all the time anyway and should be acknowledged. This is a two-way process as you will give the consultant feedback about what they are doing, and this will be giving you feedback about how you are managing the consultancy.

• Participant Feedback

The views of participants can be collected as part of the formative evaluation reviews or for the end-of-consultancy evaluation. You will need to ensure that the views of participants from different levels in the organisation and with different personal perspectives are collected. The design of evaluation methods will depend on the nature of the consultancy task but some simple techniques that have been used include:

Before-And-After Questionnaires
- Participants filling in a questionnaire before the consultancy starts, and after the consultancy has finished, describing their view of the issues that the consultancy is seeking to address. The replies are collated and an analysis made of the results. This is a summative evaluation method.

Intervention Review Sheets
- Participants filling in a review sheet at the end of an interview, discussion or event with the consultant describing how they felt about what had happened. These are collated and analysed. Formative evaluation.

Diary Review Sheets
- Participants filling in a diary review sheet that describes on a weekly or monthly basis their perception of change or development that is happening during and after the consultancy. This can be used for both formative and summative evaluation.

Talking Wall
- Participants filling in a talking wall about the consultancy. A number of sentences for completion are written on each of a number of flipchart sheets:
  "What I valued most about the consultancy was . . ."
  "Something I would have liked done different was . . ."
  "The main thing I am taking away as a result of the consultancy is . . ."
  "My view of the role played by the consultant is that . . ."
  This is most often used as a summative evaluation method.

Sample Interviews
- A sample of participants are interviewed to find out their views of the experience and their perception of the changes that have taken place. This can be formative or summative depending on when it takes place.

• User Feedback

The views of people or agencies affected by the consultancy should also be collected using simple information gathering methods. These can include:

- A postal questionnaire to agencies seeking their reactions to your new ways of doing things.
- A tick-the-box wall chart for users of a centre to assess whether they have noticed any changes and to gather their opinions.
- A management committee review meeting that receives presentations from staff about action they have taken and the effects these have had.
- An 'opinion poll' survey of users conducted by staff.
- A seminar to which other agencies or users are invited to contribute views.

• Consultant's Feedback

The consultants themselves will have views on the product, the process and the outcomes of the consultancy. You will have been gaining that feedback on a regular basis during the consultancy but you could ask consultants to give a final response at the end that sums up their evaluation of the work.

What are Your Options If It Goes Wrong?

Hopefully you will not be in a position of using a consultant who fails to do the work or does the work in ways that seriously damage your organisation.

The more care you take in choosing a consultant, agreeing a contract, working jointly or regularly reviewing how it is proceeding should ensure that any problems about the consultancy are ironed out at the earliest possible stages.

● Learn From The Experience

Both you and the consultant you use will know that not everything will turn out perfectly. Sometimes things just don't seem to work no matter how hard you and they have tried. But even then, all is not lost. If changes can't be made as you go along, you should use an unsuccessful experience as an opportunity for learning. Have a good look at every stage in the process and identify why things didn't work out the way you hoped.

- Was using a consultant the wrong way to tackle the problem in the first place?
- Did you, with hindsight, use a consultant who didn't have the necessary skills or share similar values?
- Was something important not discussed at the contracting meeting?
- Was there a communication breakdown during the information gathering/ diagnosis phase?

The consultant too should use an unsuccessful consultancy as a learning experience. Their confidence in their own abilities and skills will have taken a knock and they might welcome an honest and two-way appraisal of where things didn't go as they expected. An open and joint review of something that has not gone well might be painful but will be of much more value to all concerned.

● Withholding Payment

Whilst it is common practice and reasonable to make a final consultancy payment dependent on receiving a final report, it is not appropriate to withhold payment for a report you do not agree with.

The values and principles of consultancy work both ways. If a consultant does not do the work, then they cannot expect to be paid. But if they do the work in ways you are unhappy about, then you must discuss this with the consultant when it happens and negotiate changes. It is unreasonable to leave your complaints until the end and then refuse to pay.

> One consultant was asked to give an 'honest, warts 'n all account' of what a small community project *was* doing and what they *should be* doing. The outcome reflected the lack of direction, financial management and internal conflict and included criticism of staff and management. The report was used by the funding body as one reason for closing the project down. The project co-ordinator ran off with the remaining bank balance and no-one would accept responsibility for paying the consultant who never received his fee or expenses.

● Sue The Consultant

Ultimately if a consultant gives you advice that is legally wrong and in acting upon it you suffer damage, you can sue for negligence: for example, if you adopted a consultant's advice on equal opportunities in recruitment and it was then proven at a tribunal that you unfairly discriminated against someone on the basis of that advice.

But proving negligence is very difficult, costly and time-consuming. However, some consultants are insured against negligence — particularly those who, like accountants and lawyers, give specialist advice related to legal matters such as constitution or employment law.

EVALUATING CONSULTANCY
KEY POINTS

1. Evaluation is the process by which a judgement is made about the value of a consultancy. It should be an integral part of the consultancy contract.

2. The two reasons for evaluating a consultancy are:
   - to help change and develop the consultancy as it goes along — formative evaluation.
   - to assess at the end whether the outcomes and processes of the consultancy achieved what was intended — summative evaluation.

3. There are three aspects of consultancy to evaluate:

   1. The product. eg. a report on new ways of working with young people who have offended.
   2. The process. eg. interviews with young people who have offended.
   3. The outcomes — changes to what you do. eg. staff training in new ways of working with young people;
      - the results of these changes. eg. young people commit less serious offences.

4. Evaluation methods include:

   - Progress reviews
   - Participation feedback through:
     - before-and-after questionnaires
     - intervention review sheets
     - diary review sheets
     - talking wall
     - sample interviews
   - User feedback through:
     - postal questionnaires
     - tick-the-box wall charts
     - 'opinion poll' surveys
     - committee decision
   - Consultant's feedback

5. Not all consultancy will be successful. But every consultancy gives opportunities for learning from the experience both for you and the consultant. Ultimately you have the options of withholding payment and suing the consultant if you are extremely dissatisfied or damaged by the work of a consultant.

Appendices

A Long Tender

A Short Tender

A Pre-Meeting Questionnaire

A Survey Questionnaire

A Simple Diagnostic Tool for Reviewing Small Voluntary Organisations

A Consultancy Evaluation Form

References and Further Reading

Sources of Further Information

Appendix one

Example of a Long Tender for a 60-day Strategic Review

COMMUNITY ACTION NETWORK
STRATEGIC REVIEW 1990
TENDER BY 'PROGRESS'

Contents

1. Introduction
2. Need For the Review
3. 'Progress'
   - **Experience and Values**
   - **Motivation**
   - **Partnership**
4. Purpose and focus of the Review
5. Review Methodology
   - **General Approach**
   - **Phase 1 Preparation**
   - **Phase 2 Information Gathering**
   - **Phase 3 Interim Report**
   - **Phase 4 Exploring Choices and Directions**
   - **Phase 5 Final Report**
   - **Review Schedule Summary**
6. Review Outcome
7. Budget
8. Roles
   - **Progress**
   - **Community Action Network**
   - **Review Group**
9. References

Strategic Review 1990

1. INTRODUCTION

This paper outlines a tender by 'Progress' to undertake an independent strategic review of Community Action Network. It is based upon the Review Paper prepared for the CAN committee and the brief summary explaining why the review is felt to be necessary. It also reflects meetings with the Head of Department and other HQ staff.

2. NEED FOR THE REVIEW

Community Action Network has identified the need to undertake a fundamental review of all aspects of its practice, policy and management. The key elements identified as prompting the need for a review are:

- Relying on tradition and reputation to attract people rather than adapting structures and programmes to reach the needs and expectations of people who inevitably have changed.
- Needing to develop ways of working that will attract and retain people from all sectors of the community, especially those in different age ranges.
- Wanting to build on excellent examples of current Community Action Network provision to become the national standard.
- Needing to alter attitudes and acquire commitment in order to undertake other areas of community action.

3. 'PROGRESS'

Experience and Values Progress is an independent and experienced group of consultants and trainers established in the early 1980s to work with statutory and voluntary agencies throughout the UK. One of the main areas of our work has been to improve the quality of practice, policy and management of Community Action organisations. 'Progress' services include conducting reviews, management consultancy, advising on policy development, training and producing publications.

Like Community Action Network, we place a high value on respecting people as individuals and seeking to achieve equality of opportunity and empowerment for people.

Motivation The strategic development of Community Action Network is an exciting prospect for the whole of community development in the UK. Community Action Network is a large and strategically important community work organisation that affects the lives and development of many people. It is an agency with significant influence in the UK voluntary and statutory community development sectors.

This review and the subsèquent Strategic Development Plan for Community Action Network will have far-reaching effects for the communities it serves. It will also have a significant impact upon a wide range of other local and national community development agencies.

Partnership We welcome the opportunity to work with Community Action Network to assist the organisation to play a much greater role in responding to the needs of disadvantaged communities in the UK, and to influence the work of others concerned with community development.

In conducting this independent review we will be concerned to work in partnership with Community Action Network in order to ensure ownership and a commitment to the outcomes.

We believe we have the values, knowledge, experience and motivation to assist Community Action Network undertake a strategic review that will establish its future direction and management in the 1990s and beyond.

4. PURPOSE AND FOCUS OF THE REVIEW

Purpose   The purpose of the review is to develop a 5 year strategic plan that will ensure Community Action Network is relevant to the needs and aspirations of disadvantaged communities in the 1990s and into the 21st century.

Focus   The two papers provided by Community Action Network describe the terms of reference and objectives of the review. These can be combined and summarised as four themes that will be the focus of the review:

1. **Purpose And Aims**
   To identify the overall purpose, aims and constituency of Community Action Network and the priorities for the next five years.
2. **Methods and Services**
   To examine:
   - the current, location, quality of experience, range of practice and use by different communities of Community Action Network provision;
   - exemplary practice and experience within Community Action Network upon which to build;
   - the need and potential for people in local communities to be community development workers locally, nationally and internationally;
   - the capability of and need for Community Action Network to use its recognised skills and expertise in inner cities and with the black community and other minority groups; and
   - the need and potential for using Community Action Network expertise more widely in the field of Community Development Education and to influence the development and implementation of the adult education national curriculum.
3. **Management and Leadership**
   To identify and analyse:
   - the current pattern of staffing at local levels;
   - the management systems including recruitment, supervision and support, staff development and training, planning and evaluation, fundraising, financing and resource allocation;
   - the management structure and the allocation of roles and responsibilities throughout;
   - the decision and policy making processes and structures with particular reference to communities' participation.
4. **Public and Inter-Agency Relations**
   To explore:
   - the image of Community Action Network among disadvantaged groups and other agencies including type of activities, cross cultural aspects and relevance;
   - the relationship of Community Action Network to other voluntary and statutory community work agencies in terms of practice, provision and partnership arrangements.

5. REVIEW METHODOLOGY

General Approach   A final report will be produced by Progress that gives an independent and objective review of Community Action Network. However, it is important that the review process encourages 'ownership' of the outcome by the organisation. To that end people throughout the organisation will have the opportunity to contribute their views and to discuss the preliminary and final outcomes of the review.

The review will take place in a series of phases as summarised below:

Phase 1	Preparation Review Group	April 1990 May
Phase 2	Information Gathering	May–August
Phase 3	Interim Report Review Group	September 1990
Phase 4	Exploring The Options Council Meeting	October/November 1990
Phase 5	Draft Report Review Group Final Report Council Meeting	December 1990 January 1991

Phase 1: Preparation April 1990

1.1 Clarification and agreement of the detailed terms of reference and boundaries for the review, the review methods, the roles and expectations, and the schedule.

1.2 Initial identification of the key issues and questions. These will be amended as the quantitative and qualitative data is gathered. Phases 1.1 and 1.2 will be undertaken at the first meeting of the Review Group.

1.3 Preparation for data collection including designing the questionnaire and interviews, agreeing topics for group discussion, identifying examples of practice to be examined in more detail and agreeing access to existing records and materials.

1.4 Communication throughout the organisation about the review process, timetable and how people will be involved.

Phase 2: Information Gathering May–August 1990

A variety of information gathering methods will be used in order to collect both quantitative and qualitative data, and to avoid relying on one method or source for analysis.

Emphasis will also be placed upon methods that involve the staff in organising and conducting elements of the information gathering process as well as providing data and giving their views.

It is important that people in local communities have direct as well as indirect (ie. through local workers) ways of contributing to the review. The input from local communities is as an integral part of the process and is shown as such in the information gathering methods below.

2.1 Area Meetings

The countries of Scotland, Wales and Northern Ireland, and to a lesser extent the four areas of England have distinct cultural identities that need to be reflected in the review.

Progress will spend one day in each of the 8 areas:

East	Scotland
West	Northern Ireland
North	Wales
South	London

These are large geographical areas each of which contain a number of regions which in turn have many branches and groups. The purpose of the days will be to discuss the main themes of the review face-to-face with people at different levels in the organisation including local people, community workers, Branch Directors and Regional Officers. People will be encouraged to have preparatory discussions in their branches and regions prior to the area meetings in order to increase the numbers able to make an active contribution and to encourage a wider range of discussion. The days will be carefully structured to ensure the focus is kept on the points of most relevance to the review.

We will consult with the appropriate staff to discuss how to make best use of the area meetings. The days could be structured as a single event to which a wide group is invited. Alternatively they could be organised as a series of small workshops that different groups of people attend at different times.

2.2 Interviews With External Agencies

A number of external agencies will be interviewed to gather views and information. Example of agencies to be included are:

- Government Departments such as the DES, Scottish Office, the Northern Ireland Office and HMI.
- Community development umbrella bodies in the four countries.
- Councils For Voluntary Service in inner city areas.
- Black and Asian organisations.
- Relevant national voluntary organisations.
- Disabled People's organisations.
- Women's organisations.

2.3 Internal Interviews

Views and information will be gathered through interviews from various parts of Community Action Network including:

- Individual HQ staff
- Staff within Community Action Network with different personal perspectives
- Committee members within Community Action Network.

2.4 Internal Group Discussion

Each local group will be asked to hold a discussion with their members of up to six key questions and each Branch to collate a summary of the results. We would like this to be done with people from local communities.

In addition, Progress will:

- Attend a meeting of the Senior Management Team to facilitate a discussion on the future of Community Action Network.
- Facilitate a one-day seminar on the review for the HQ staff and UK Director.
- Facilitate a meeting of the National Community Action Forum.
- Attend meeting of the Black Worker's Forum and the Women Worker's Forum

2.5 Questionnaire

A short questionnaire will be sent to each Branch to be completed by the local community work officer after consultation with people in their local branch. The process of discussion within the branches needed to complete the questionnaire is itself an important part of the review that will encourage debate, contributions and ownership of the outcomes.

2.6 Written Submissions

In addition to the questionnaire the community work offices of each branch will be invited to make a factual written submission to the review that describes:

(a) the current pattern of types of community action work in the branch;
(b) the staffing structure in the branch and the roles played by different people;
(c) how local people are involved in decision and policy making;
(d) how the branch relates to other community work providers.

A common format will be provided on which to make these submissions.

2.7 Reading

A number of key documents will be read and analysed. This list is not complete but will include:

- Branch annual reports
- Published materials, eg. community action packs
- Training materials
- Policy statements
- Community Action National Newsheets
- Salary structures
- Government policy statements on Community Development.

2.8 Statistical Data

We will require access to statistical data already collected by Community Action Network including:

- Distribution of UK groups
- Attendance at UK Community Action groups by age and sex
- Full/part-time and voluntary staffing of UK groups.

Other relevant statistical data may be sought if it is available.

Phase 3 Interim Report September 1990

At the end of the information gathering phase, an interim report will be produced that summarises the key findings, analyses the implications, and draws out options for the future for all the areas covered by the review. In a strategic review of this kind it is important to have a two-stage process for interpreting the findings and identifying and discussing options before a final report is made.

   The interim report will be presented to the Review Group for discussion and comment.

Phase 4 Exploring Choices and Directions October/November 1990

The summary and the options outlined in the interim report for the strategic future of Community Action Network will be discussed widely within the organisation.

   This is a crucial phase involving exploration of the options in depth, discussion of the implications, opportunity for feelings to be expressed and enabling groups to feel they have had a real say in the outcome. We will assist the staff to plan this process and will ourselves facilitate half-day discussions of the interim report in each of the regions and within Headquarters.

   The interim report could also be given consideration at a full meeting of the National Committee.

Phase 5 Final Report December 1990/January 1991

The final report will be produced in two stages. A draft will be written taking into account the feedback from comments on the interim report. This will be discussed at a meeting of the review group. The final report will be produced in time for discussion by the Senior Management Team at National Head-quarters so that decisions can be made at the January 1991 meeting of the National Committee.

6. THE REVIEW OUTCOME

a) The review report will seek to reflect the strategic nature of the task. In practice this means that a relatively large amount of information is collected and then narrowed or distilled into the key findings, issues and options.

It is important that the appropriate level of detail is included at the interim and final report stages. We envisage that the interim report will be no more than 20 pages and the final report no more than 60 pages in length.

b) The less visible but no less important outcome of the review is that there is ownership and commitment to the 5 year strategic plan that is produced at its conclusion.

c) In the longer term the review should result in

- more involvement of people from all sections of the community especially those in different age ranges.
- existing examples of excellent practice becoming the national standard.
- new attitudes and commitment among staff and volunteers to undertake a wider range of areas of community action.

Budget Notes

1. The allocation of days to each task is an estimate based on previous experience of large and strategic reviews of this kind. This may be amended as the review progresses subject to discussion and agreement with the Head of Department.
2. The travel and subsistence costs are an estimate based on second class rail and 41p per mile car usage. The extent to which air travel is required is unclear so the cost of air fares will be in addition to this budget subject to agreement with the Head of Department. All travel and subsistence costs will be carefully monitored and reported regularly.
3. The cost of printing/photocopying and posting questionnaires or other material associated with the review will be borne by Community Action Network.
4. The lead consultant will attend the three one-day meetings of the Review Group and the other consultants will contribute as appropriate.
5. VAT at the rate prevailing on the day of invoice is chargeable on all costs.

8. ROLES

1. Progress

Three consultants from Progress will be involved in the review. This is designed to create the best balance of knowledge, experience and skills, a wide geographical spread and a mixed gender team. This team approach is one that we have successfully adopted elsewhere and provides both an internal sounding board and mutual support for the consultants during the review. Details about the consultants are provided separately and Vicky will be the lead consultant for the review.

2. Community Action Network

Community Action Network Staff
Community Action Network staff will be involved in a number of ways:

Budget

Phase	Task	Consultancy Days	Fee	Travel/ Subsistence	Total
1	Review Group Preparation Work	5	1250	225	1475
2	Regional Meetings:	8	2000	600	2600
	External Interviews:	3	750	300	1050
	Internal Interviews:	5	1250	500	1750
	Group Discussions:	3	750	225	975
	Questionnaires:	2	500	–	500
	Reading: Statistical Data: Written Submissions:	4	1000	–	1000
3	Interim Report & Review Group:	8	2000	450	2450
4	Exploring Options:	5	1250	375	1625
5	First Draft: Review Group: Final Report:	14	3500	450	3950
	Sub-Total:	57	14250	3125	17375
	Typing				250
	Post and Phone				200
				TOTAL	17825

- organising regional and other meetings
- making written submissions
- completing questionnaires
- participating in interviews and group discussions
- providing statistical and other information
- attending Review Group meetings
- printing and distributing information etc.

3. Review Group

The consultants will be supported at key stages of the review process by an internal Review Group, the membership of which is described in the review paper agreed by the National Committee. The Review Group will be responsible for monitoring the progress of the review and evaluating the success of the review in achieving its objectives.

4. Accountability

The final report will be presented to the Director, Community Action Network. Day-to-day liaison will be with the Head of Department. Progress will undertake the bulk of the data collection and analysis, and will produce the final report. Final decisions on the report will rest solely with Progress. Community Action Network will then draw up a strategic plan using the findings of the report to inform its decision making.

9. REFERENCES

References for Progress and the three consultants involved in the review are provided separately.

Appendix two

Example of a Short Tender for a Three day Team Review Process

COMMUNITY ACTION NETWORK
TEAM REVIEW AND DEVELOPMENT
TENDER BY 'PROGRESS'

- **Introduction**

This proposal for a three-day team review and development process for the staff of CAN is based on an initial meeting with the project coordinator.

It is intended to be the basis for a discussion with the whole team on whether to proceed and, if so, to agree the details of the consultancy process.

- **Purpose and Focus**

The aims of the team review and development process will be:

- to identify ways of overcoming obstacles to greater user involvement in the overall running of the organisation;
- to identify ways of developing roles, workloads and tasks of staff that are congruent with greater user involvement and working more as a team;
- to plan practical improvements to the way the staff work together as a team (e.g. meetings, decision making and so on).

- **Overall Approach**

The consultant will act as facilitator to the CAN staff assisting them to achieve the agreed aims. He will draw on his own knowledge and experience as appropriate and use methods of working with the team that might be used in turn by staff with the people they serve. Emphasis will be given on empowering people individually and as a team, ensuring equality of opportunity and developing independence.

- **Values**

Progress is an independent and experienced group of consultants and trainers established in the early 1980s, to work with statutory and voluntary agencies throughout the UK. We place a high value on respecting people as individuals, on seeking to address issues of social equality and on empowering people. Like CAN, we believe in user involvement and have experience of putting this into practice. We believe we have the knowledge, commitment and experience to assist CAN develop this approach to their work.

- **Methodology**

The process will include:

1. A preliminary meeting between the team and the consultant to agree the specific objectives and methods for the review.
2. Staff completing and returning a confidential questionnaire (attached) to the consultant prior to an initial two-day event.
3. Staff interviewing members of the committee and users to find out their expectations about user involvement in the organisation.
4. Two days working together with the consultant on the issues resulting in specific outcomes to be put into practice. This will take place locally but at a venue away from the CAN office.
5. Two subsequent half-days with the consultant reviewing progress three months and six months after the initial two days.

• Product

The individual questionnaires will remain completely confidential to the consultant but a summary of the key issues identified will be produced and will form the basis of the work over the two days. A written report of the outcome of the two days will also be produced that will be referred to in the subsequent half-day review meetings.

• Support and Involvement of the Organisation

All staff will be expected to participate in the process including completing the questionnaire, interviewing committee members and users, attending the initial two-days and the two review sessions.

• Timetable

It is envisaged that the preliminary meeting and preparation would take place in September/early October; and the two days meeting in late October. The review meetings will take place in January and April.

• Roles, Accountability and Confidentiality

The role of staff and committee members in the process is described above. The consultant is accountable to the project co-ordinator and through her to the chair of the committee. The written report of the two days will be made available to all staff, and after consultation with staff, to the committee.

• Budget

The cost of using the consultant is:

Fees:	£200 per day @ 3 days	£600.00
Travel and Subsistence and Administration	up to a maximum of £30	30.00
	sub-total	630.00
VAT @ 15%	sub-total	94.50
	TOTAL:	£724.50

Note

- Additional costs to be borne by CAN will include room hire, and subsistence for staff.
- VAT will be chargeable at the rate prevailing on the day of invoice.

• The Consultant

The consultant will be J. Smith of Progress

Appendix three

A Pre-Meeting Questionnaire

CONFIDENTIAL

COMMUNITY ACTION NETWORK
TEAM REVIEW AND DEVELOPMENT

This is a confidential questionnaire to help me plan the two-day team review and development process in October 1990. Please fill in brief answers to the questions below and return the form to me, Jenny Smith, by no later than Friday 12th October 1990.

Name:

Role/Job:

1. What do you think are the main obstacles to greater user involvement in the day-to-day work and overall running of CAN?

2. What particular aspects of roles, workloads and tasks among staff are you concerned to have covered during the two days?

3. What particular systems, or meetings, or other aspects of the way the organisation is run would you like to see improved?

4. Complete the sentence: "By the end of the two days I hope we will have:

   •

   •

   •

5. Any other comments about the content or the processes to be covered on the two days.

Many thanks for filling this in.
Don't forget to send it off — deadline 12th October 1990!

Appendix four

A Survey Questionnaire

COMMUNITY ACTION NETWORK REVIEW
YOUNG PEOPLE'S QUESTIONNAIRE

Community Action Network is a project that assists people to do something about problems or issues they face in the community. It provides information, advice and support to people as individuals or in groups who want to take action on something that concerns them. CAN has helped local people to do things for themselves and to have a greater influence with others, such as the Council and local businesses, who affect their lives.

The questionnaire is anonymous.

• Information About You

This questionnaire is anonymous but to help us analyse the results please answer these questions about yourself.

1) Age:

2) Male _____ Female _____ (please tick)

3) How would you describe yourself:

(please tick) White _____ Afro-Caribbean _____ Asian _____

Other _____ (please describe) _____

Would you describe yourself as having a disability? Yes/No

If 'Yes', please specify: _____

• Information about CAN

1) Have you heard of Community Action Network? YES / NO

2) If you have had contact with Community Action Network in any way, how good did you think it was?

a) I had contact with Community Action Network about: _____

b) It was: very poor ___ very good ____ poor ___ satisfactory _____
good _____

3) Community Action Network provides information, advice and support for young people who want to take action on issues of concern to them in the community.

   a) When do you think it should be open? – Days of the week:
                                                   – Time of the day:

   b) Community Action Network is based in the centre of the town. In addition to this, where else would it be a good idea to provide such information, advice and support for young people?

   c) What else do you think Community Action Network should provide for young people?

4) What stops you from getting information, advice or support from Community Action Network?

5) Community Action Network wants more young people to get involved in making decisions about what goes on. What do you think would be the best way to do this:

                                      Please Tick

- A public meeting open to all young people locally
- Delegates from youth clubs locally come to a meeting
- Delegates from schools in the area come to a meeting
- Regular questionnaires to young people
- Other ideas:
  -
  -

6) Put a circle around the SIX issues or problems in the community that are of most importance to you:

        Work   Relationships   Fitness

   Drink   Sexism   School Problems   Benefits

     Racism Music   Housing   Hobbies   Abuse

   Environment   Legal Rights   Access

    Trouble With The Law   Money

     Health   Drugs   Travel

   Discrimination   Entertainment

Thank you for filling in this questionnaire.

Appendix five

A Simple Diagnostic Tool for Reviewing Small Voluntary Organisations

Creating a Secure and Successful Future

● Introduction

This questionnaire has been designed to help you to identify priority areas needing work in your organisation, in order to create a secure and successful future.

The idea is to assist your thinking rather than to come up with a picture of 'truth' of your organisation. It should lead on to further discussion and debate.

You may well want to answer 'it depends' to many of the questions. Try to take a broad perspective and answer 'generally . . .'. Your answers should reflect the level of need for further work in this area. Suggestions/amendments to the exercise are always welcome.

● What To Do:

1. Complete the *Organisational Review Questionnaire* on your own.
   15–20 mins.

2. Calculate your results and plot them onto the *Organisational Review Profile* (steps 1–4).
   10 mins.

3. When you've done steps 1–4, discuss and compare your results with that of others in the organisation. You could compile one large profile using the scores of everyone taking part.

4. Discuss:

   1. Do we have a shared analysis of the areas going well and those needing most attention? If not, why do we differ? Does this profile match what we know from our experience, what we observe and other information?

   2. Having agreed the areas you need to work on, what do you think is causing the problems? The original questions on this area might give you some starting points for this analysis .

   3. What ways of resolving the problems you have identified could be developed?

Organisational Review Questionnaire

● SCORING SYSTEM

Read the 76 statements and give each one a 'score' as shown below. Write the scores on the scoring sheet attached. Do not take too long scoring each statement – the whole lot should take 15–20 minutes maximum!

1. Do not agree at all.
2. Agree to a very limited extent.
3. Agree to some extent.
4. Agree this is generally the case.
5. Complete agreement.

If you don't know, score (1).

● ORGANISATIONAL REVIEW QUESTIONNAIRE

1. People in the organisation use their time well.
2. Our organisation has clear aims and methods of working.
3. People know a number of planning techniques.
4. The organisation has a clear overall fundraising strategy.
5. The task of fundraising has been clearly allocated.
6. We use a variety of methods for fundraising.
7. There is an effective financial planning and control system.
8. People understand how to evaluate the work of the organisation.
9. We have good relationships with agencies we seek to influence.
10. We are good at promoting the benefits of what we do.
11. People have one-to-one supervision sessions regularly.
12. There is a full induction system for new people in the organisation.
13. Staff are encouraged to take up training opportunities.
14. There are clear procedures for recruitment and selection of staff, volunteers and committee members.
15. The membership of our management committee includes the skills that are needed.
16. People in our organisation are good at giving and receiving feedback.
17. The predominant management style used suits our organisation.
18. Communication systems amongst staff work well.
19. Roles and responsibilities of different staff members are clear.
20. People in the organisation spend their time on important issues.
21. There is a clear forward plan for the future of the organisation.
22. People use different planning techniques to suit different needs.
23. We are clear about what will be our future sources of fundraising.
24. Our fundraising planning is well organised.
25. Our fundraising is done professionally and skilfully.
26. Our current finances are in a healthy state.
27. There is a clear system for evaluating the work.
28. Other organisations have an accurate idea about our aims and methods of working.
29. We have good working relationships with the press, TV, and radio.
30. People know who to turn to for managerial and non-managerial support and advice.
31. By the end of their first month, new staff have a good idea of how the organisation works.
32. There is a training budget for staff.
33. A written policy exists on what to do when a post falls vacant and is to be filled.

34. The roles of management committee members are clear to them.
35. People in our organisation negotiate well.
36. There is a positive climate in our staff team.
37. Filing and record-keeping systems are efficient.
38. People have the skills to carry out their roles.
39. People in the organisation book in time for preparation.
40. The organisation has a well thought through strategy for key areas of future development.
41. All staff use planning techniques at some level.
42. Our fundraising strategy is directly linked to our development plan.
43. Fundraising is seen as an important role in the organisation.
44. We use appropriate methods for fundraising.
45. We have a secure financial base for the future.
46. Evaluation is used to help improve practice and plan the way forward.
47. The mechanisms we use for inter-agency liaison are effective.
48. Our publicity material is well presented and reflects our values.
49. People welcome the chance to regularly review their work with someone else.
50. Everyone is clear about what they have to do when someone new starts work.
51. Time is set aside for team training.
52. The recruitment and selection procedures take full account of equal opportunities.
53. The staff/management committee relationship is good.
54. People use effective procedures for managing conflict.
55. Team meetings work well.
56. Sharing of information is encouraged in our organisation.
57. The way work is allocated is appropriate.
58. People in the organisation don't waste time.
59. There is a clear system for overall forward planning in the organisation.
60. Planning involves people throughout the organisation.
61. Our overall fundraising strategy is well thought through and achievable.
62. It is clear what role the management committee has for fundraising.
63. Our fundraising methods achieve good results.
64. The organisation has got to grips with its finances.
65. Staff have a positive attitude to evaluating their work.
66. We have good personal contact with key people in other agencies.
67. Our publicity material avoids stereotypes.
68. There is a written agreement about supervision in the organisation.
69. New staff have a full review of their work after six months.
70. We have an agreed system for identifying and meeting people's training needs.
71. It is clear who is involved in the recruitment and selection of new people into the organisation.
72. The management committee meetings work well.
73. People have a high level of skill in communicating effectively with each other.
74. It is clear which people can make decisions.
75. People receive the information they need to do their jobs well.
76. People have realistic expectations of each other.

● SCORE SHEET

1	20	39	58	A	_____
2	21	40	59	B	_____
3	22	41	60	C	_____
4	23	42	61	D	_____
5	24	43	62	E	_____
6	25	44	63	F	_____
7	26	45	64	G	_____
8	27	46	65	H	_____
9	28	47	66	I	_____
10	29	48	67	J	_____
11	30	49	68	K	_____
12	31	50	69	L	_____
13	32	51	70	M	_____
14	33	52	71	N	_____
15	34	53	72	O	_____
16	35	54	73	P	_____
17	36	55	74	Q	_____
18	37	56	75	R	_____
19	38	57	76	S	_____

● PLOTTING THE RESULTS TO CREATE AN ORGANISATIONAL PROFILE

1. Add up your scores across the rows, e. g.

    First Row   Total
       1. (4) + 20. (3) + 39. (5) + 58. (3) = (15) A

    Second Row
       2. (1) + 21. (2) + 40. (2) + 59. (1) = (6) B
          etc.

2. Plot your total scores on the profile sheet.

    - The total in the *first row* is plotted onto the first column (A) on the graph profile (eg. (15) is the score to be marked on the first column (Column A).)

    - The total in the *second row* is plotted onto the second column (Column B) on the graph profile. (Eg. (6) is the score to be marked on the second column (Column B) etc.)

3. Now join the dots! You have created an organisational review profile. The areas where you have high scores (high points on the profile) are those which are going relatively well.

    The areas where you have low scores are those which appear to need most attention.

4. The graph shows a worked example profile of an organisation that needs to work on:

    - Time Management
    - Management of Fundraising
    - Supervision and Support
    - Management Committee Development
    - Teamwork

ORGANISATIONAL REVIEW PROFILE

Col	Category	Sub-category	Score scale
A	PLANNING	TIME MANAGEMENT	4–20
B	PLANNING	FORWARD PLANS AND STRATEGIES	4–20
C	PLANNING	PLANNING TECHNIQUES	4–20
D	FUNDING	OVERALL FUNDRAISING STRATEGY	4–20
E	FUNDING	MANAGEMENT OF FUNDRAISING	4–20
F	FUNDING	FUNDRAISING SKILLS AND METHODS	4–20
G	FUNDING	FINANCES	4–20
H	EVALUATION	EVALUATION	4–20
I	PUBLIC RELATIONS	EXTERNAL RELATIONSHIPS	4–20
J	PUBLIC RELATIONS	P.R. SKILLS & METHODS	4–20
K	STAFF SUPPORT & DEVELOPMENT	SUPERVISION & SUPPORT	4–20
L	STAFF SUPPORT & DEVELOPMENT	INDUCTION	4–20
M	STAFF SUPPORT & DEVELOPMENT	TRAINING	4–20
N	STAFF SUPPORT & DEVELOPMENT	RECRUITMENT SELECTION	4–20
O	M/MENT COMM.	MANAGEMENT COMMITTEE	4–20
P	INTER-PERSONAL SKILLS	INTERPERSONAL SKILLS	4–20
Q	MANAGEMENT SYSTEMS	TEAMWORK	4–20
R	MANAGEMENT SYSTEMS	INFORMATION FLOW	4–20
S	MANAGEMENT SYSTEMS	ROLES & RESPONSIBILITIES	4–20

SCORE: 20 19 18 17 16 15 14 13 12 11 10 9 8 7 6 5 4

Name of your Organisation ....

Person Completing the Profile ....

Date ....

ORGANISATIONAL REVIEW PROFILE

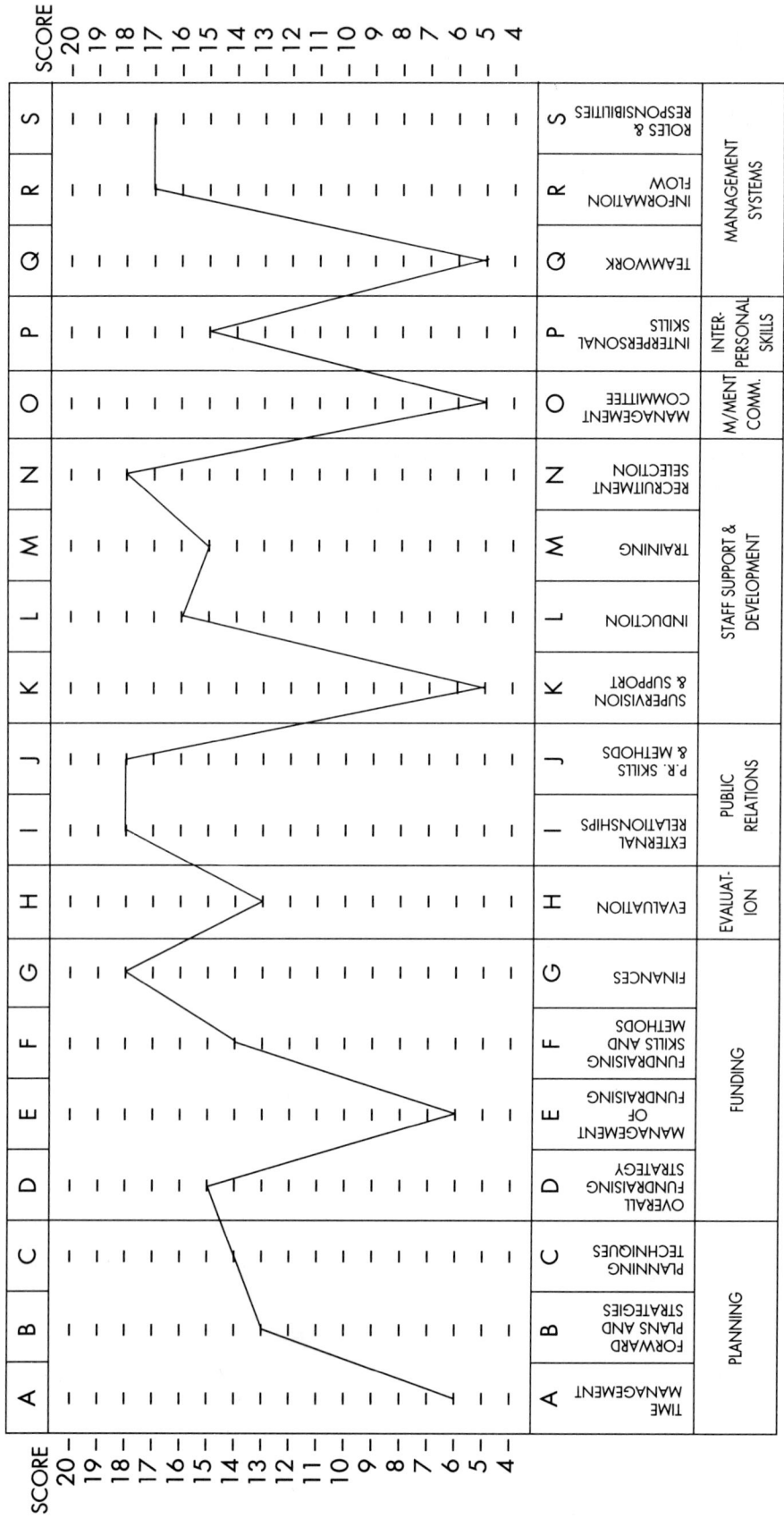

SCORE: 20 19 18 17 16 15 14 13 12 11 10 9 8 7 6 5 4

Col	Category	System
A	TIME MANAGEMENT	PLANNING
B	FORWARD PLANS AND STRATEGIES	PLANNING
C	PLANNING TECHNIQUES	PLANNING
D	OVERALL FUNDRAISING STRATEGY	FUNDING
E	MANAGEMENT OF FUNDRAISING	FUNDING
F	FUNDRAISING SKILLS AND METHODS	FUNDING
G	FINANCES	FUNDING
H	EVALUATION	EVALUAT-ION
I	EXTERNAL RELATIONSHIPS	PUBLIC RELATIONS
J	P.R. SKILLS & METHODS	PUBLIC RELATIONS
K	SUPERVISION & SUPPORT	STAFF SUPPORT & DEVELOPMENT
L	INDUCTION	STAFF SUPPORT & DEVELOPMENT
M	TRAINING	STAFF SUPPORT & DEVELOPMENT
N	RECRUITMENT SELECTION	STAFF SUPPORT & DEVELOPMENT
O	MANAGEMENT COMMITTEE	M/MENT COMM.
P	INTERPERSONAL SKILLS	INTER-PERSONAL SKILLS
Q	TEAMWORK	MANAGEMENT SYSTEMS
R	INFORMATION FLOW	MANAGEMENT SYSTEMS
S	ROLES & RESPONSIBILITIES	MANAGEMENT SYSTEMS

SCORE: 20 19 18 17 16 15 14 13 12 11 10 9 8 7 6 5 4

Name of your Organisation ....

Person Completing the Profile ....

Date ....

Appendix
six

A Consultancy Evaluation Form

CONSULTANCY EVALUATION
FORM

● **Purpose**

This form is to enable us to monitor reaction to work that we have done, in order to maintain and develop the quality of our practice. This evaluation form may refer to work which is still progressing, and is another method to ensure that our ongoing work is meeting people's needs.

Please will you complete the form and return to the address given. The comments will be strictly confidential and will form the basis for discussions and action concerning our practice.

1. Consultant(s) / Trainer(s) involved:

2. Your organisation:

3. Your name:

4. Your role in the contract:

5. Brief description of the contract: (eg. long-term strategic review, 2-day team building event, practice development consultancy etc.)

6. Do you have any comments about the nature of contract and how it was agreed?

7. What, if anything, has happened as a result of the contract? (please be as specific as possible)
*Changes in work programme,   Outcomes arising from
style, structure etc.   these changes*

8. What did you find most useful about the work:
   - methods and approaches used
   - style and skills of the consultants

9. What did you not find useful or would have liked to have done differently?

10. We aim to work towards a consistent set of values. Was a set of values apparent in any or all of the aspects of the work with you?

   YES/NO

   If 'yes', circle up to 5 words which reflect the values you saw:

   Justice   Elitist   Honest   Hierarchical

   Left-wing   Oppressive   Empowering   Devious

   Anti-sexist   Inequality   Open   Manipulative

   Equality   Racist   Co-operative   Sexist

   Anti-racist   Right-wing   Participative   Unjust

   Do you have any other comments on our values?

11. Please give your overall rating of the consultancy by marking the scale below:

   _____
   Excellent   Good   Average   Poor

   Please return this form to:

References

(1) 'Competition In the UK Management Consultancy Industry' by L. D. Reynolds MBA Dissertation, University of Bradford (unpublished)

(2) *The Consultancy Process In Action*, 2nd edition by G. Lippitt and R. Lippitt published by University Associates Inc. (1986)

(3) *Developing Supervision in Teams in Field and Residential Social Work* by Chris Payne and Tony Scott published by the National Institute for Social Work (1982)

(4) *The Tao of Leadership* by John Heider published by Wildwood House, (1985)

(5) *Flawless Consulting* by Peter Block published by University Associates Inc. (1981)

(6) *Managing Consultancy* by Rick Rogers published by the National Council for Voluntary Organisations and The Arts Council (1990)

(7) *Programme Planning and Proposal Writing* by Norton J. Kirtz published by the Grantsmanship Centre

(8) *Management Consultants: who they are and how to deal with them* Written and published by Labour Research Department (1988)

(9) *Guidelines on Charging for Management Consultancy Services* Institute of Management Consultants (1983)

(10) *Improving Work Groups: A Practical Manual* by D. Francis and D. Young published by University Associates Inc. 1979

(11) *An Experiential Approach To Organisation Development* by Harvey and Brown published by Prentice Hall (1988)

• Further Reading

'The Selection and Use of Management Development Consultants' Local Government Training Board, 1984

'Selection and Use of Management Consultants' National Audit Office, 1989.

Sources of Information

● Voluntary Umbrella Bodies

The Management Development Unit,
National Council for Voluntary Organisations,
26 Bedford Square,
London, WC1B 3HQ.
Tel: 071-636-4066

Northern Ireland Council of Voluntary Action,
127 Ormeau Road,
Belfast, BT7 1SH.
Tel: 0232-321224

Scottish Council For Voluntary Organisations,
18/19 Claremont Crescent,
Edinburgh, EH7 4HX.
Tel: 031-556-3882

Wales Council For Voluntary Action,
Llys Ifor,
Heol Crescent,
Caerffilli,
Canol Morgannwg, CF8 1XL.
Tel: 0222-869224

● Professional Bodies

Chartered Institute of Marketing,
Moor Hall,
Cookham,
Maidenhead,
Berkshire, SL6 9QH.
Tel: 06285-24922

Institute of Charity Fundraising Managers,
208 Market Towers,
Nine Elms Lane,
London, SW8 5NQ.
Tel: 071-627-3436

Institute of Management Consultants (IMC),
32-33 Hatton Garden,
London, EC1N 8DL.
Tel: 071-242-1803

Management Consultancies Association (MCA),
11 West Halkin Street,
London, SW1X 8JL.
Tel: 071-235-3897

● Directories

African, Caribbean and Asian Trainers Directory
Published by London Voluntary Services Council,
Available from African Caribbean Development Unit,
68 Chalton Street,
London NW1 1JR.
Tel: 071-388-0241

Directory of Equal Opportunity Consultants and Trainers
Published by Limbert Spencer Consultancy,
Putteridge Bury,
Hitchin Road,
Luton LU2 8LE.
Tel: 0582-487603

Directory of Management Development Consultants
Published by the Association for Management Education and Development —
AMED,
Premier House,
77 Oxford Street,
London W1R 1RB.

Directory of Trainers and Consultants
Published by the Consortium on Opportunities for Volunteering,
102 Park Village East,
London NW1 3SP

Directory of Trainers and Consultants in the Personal and Social Services
Published by Longman Group UK Ltd,
Westgate House,
Harlow, Essex CM20 1YR.
Tel: 0279-442601

Fundraising Consultants Listing for Voluntary Agencies
Published by the National Council for Voluntary Organisations,
26 Bedford Square,
London WC1B 3HQ.
Tel: 071-636-4066

Social Services Consultancy and Training Directory
Published by British Association of Social Work Trading,
BASW Trading Ltd,
16 Kent Street,
Birmingham B5 6RD.
Tel: 021-622-3911

● Unpublished Databases of Consultants are also held by:

The Management Development Team,
National Council for Voluntary Organisations,
Regent's Wharf
8 All Saints Street,
London N1 9RL.
Tel: 071-713-6161

Development Unit,
Arts Council of Great Britain,
14 Great Peter Street,
London SW1P 3NQ.
Tel: 071-333-0100

Charities Evaluation Services,
1 Motley Avenue,
Christina Street,
London EC2 4SU.
Tel: 071-613-1202

... and by some local Councils of Voluntary Service.